CHIPPENDALE

CHIPPENDALE

Nathaniel Harris

CHARTWELL
BOOKS, INC.

Overleaf: *Detail of secretaire, 1770–1773, at Harewood House, showing an ivory inlay on ebony ground*

Above: *Detail of the canopy of a George III fourposter bed at Harewood House*

This edition published by
CHARTWELL BOOKS, INC.,
a Division of BOOK SALES, INC.,
110 Enterprise Avenue,
Secaucus, New Jersey, 07094

© Octopus Books Limited 1989

ISBN 1 55521 390 1

Produced by Mandarin Offset
Printed and bound in Hong Kong

CONTENTS

Secretaire, 1770- 1773, with marquetry on satinwood, Harewood House

Chapter One

CHIPPENDALE AND HIS AGE

Chippendale was equally gifted as a craftsman and as a designer: his pattern-book, *The Gentleman and Cabinet-Maker's Director*, was a major source of inspiration and influence in furniture design. The materialist age he lived in offered ample scope for his remarkable talents: industrial development had brought great wealth to many, and Chippendale had a long list of patrons anxious to enhance their homes. His output was prolific, but although his name is synonymous with high-quality furniture, very little is known about his life, and considerable research has had to go into authenticating the many works attributed to him.

Thomas Chippendale was a master of his craft whose work is of enduring significance – and on two counts. As the author of the oddly titled *The Gentleman and Cabinet-Maker's Director* (first published in 1754) he produced the first substantial collection of furniture designs. Apart from demonstrating his genius, this provided clients and craftsmen throughout the century with a superlative pattern-book from which furniture could be chosen and made. In this way Chippendale's work did much to improve standards of both craftsmanship and taste, while also initiating a new genre without which the work of subsequent designers such as Hepplewhite and Sheraton would have been unthinkable. Moreover, as a cabinet-maker (master of a workshop making quality furniture) Chippendale himself produced furniture of the highest excellence, mastering every style to which he turned his hand and working for the aristocratic élite of his time.

This book describes both Chippendale's printed designs and his actual furniture – two subjects that overlap rather than coincide. The fame of his book designs has made these the basis of the 'Chippendale style', identifiable by its exuberant virtuoso carving; but although some of the furniture he made in this vein has survived, much more is known from a slightly later period, when he worked in a more restrained

Everybody has heard of Chippendale. He is so famous that people jokingly refer to their battered household chairs as their 'Chippendales', and in more serious vein they use the word to describe almost any 18th-century mahogany furniture whose workmanship is fanciful or intricate. For Chippendale's fame is not based on knowledge of his life and work – it is doubtful whether most people could get his first name right – but on a long-lived popular tradition not far removed from myth, conjuring up images of an elegant, sociable, supremely civilized age.

Above: *The monument to Chippendale in his birthplace, Otley, a small town in the west of Yorkshire*

style and employed a quite different set of techniques. In a sense, then, there are two equally important Chippendales, whose works in one form or another encompass all the main stylistic and technical developments over several critical decades of furniture history.

Lack of information

This is not the only unusual aspect of Chippendale's career. Although his book was recognized as a classic and his name had become legendary, by the mid-19th century information about his life and works was almost non-existent apart from a handful of unreliable traditions. As a result, there were soon furniture historians prepared to argue that his reputation had been inflated; and some held a version of that view – increasingly modified – until quite recent times. For one of the many admirable detective stories of 20th-century research concerns the piecing together of Chippendale's life story and the documented attribution of furniture to him. The process is still going on, but enough is already known for us to be sure that Chippendale was truly a master-craftman, as popular tradition always insisted.

Chippendale was fortunate in being able to work in the wealthy, taste-conscious culture of Georgian Britain, where the talented craftsman might find an abundance of creative opportunities. The beginnings of industrialism, commercial enterprise and a thriving maritime trade had made Britain rich and dynamic, without weakening the aristocratic, hierarchical nature of her

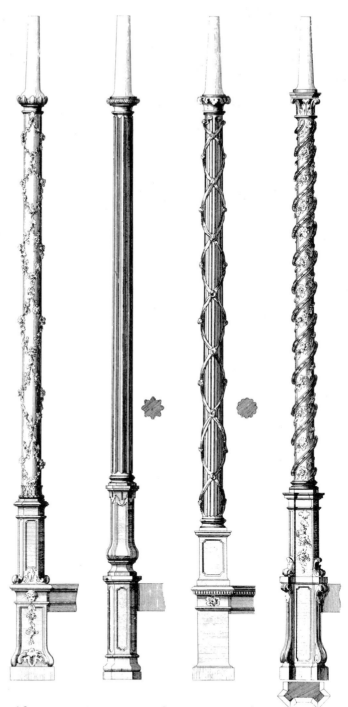

Above: *As this selection of bed pillars shows, Chippendale assumed that his patrons would pay attention to details.* The Director (1762), Pl.XXXV

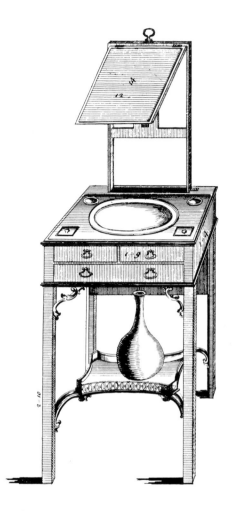

society; indeed the aristocracy participated enthusiastically in commercial and imperial expansion, and consequently enjoyed a golden age in which there was little hint of decadence. The political and religious passions of the 17th century had largely subsided, and the young and well-born could look forward to going on the Grand Tour, taking a seat in Parliament without necessarily taking much interest in politics, building and furnishing town and country houses, improving their estates and cultivating their talents and sensibilities. It was an age of show,

Left: One of six lyre-back chairs in the library at Nostell Priory

Right: A design for a washstand and mirror. The Director *(1762), Pl.LIV*

sociability and fashion, when décor was a serious matter and the ambitious provincial might make a name for himself if he managed to set up a business in the capital of taste, London. Those who could satisfy exacting clients might be asked to carry out commis-

ARCHITECTURE.

London, Printed for Robt Sayer, Printseller at the Golden Buck, near Serjeants Inn Fleet Street

sions on the grand scale, as Chippendale's surviving bills demonstrate: to the modern reader, the quantities of furniture he supplied to some families is simply amazing.

Certain less glamorous facts about Georgian society are also helpful in understanding Chippendale's career. One is his contemporaries' intense consciousness of rank and class. The hauteur which made 'the English milord' notorious abroad was also directed towards his inferiors at home — and these included 'tradesmen' such as Chippendale, who were alternately

Above: *Work in progress on a stately home. The élite in the eighteenth century were greatly concerned with outward appearances, style and fashion*

condescended to and bullied during the long intervals that elapsed between payments for their work. The client thought of him- (or her-) self as a patron dispensing bounty, and Chippendale's letters show him reacting with the required subservience and expressions of gratitude. In fact notions of patronage and 'influence' saturated 18th-century

Above: *State dining-room at Nostell Priory. The furniture is by Chippendale and the decorations by Paine. Nostell, the home of Sir Rowland Winn, is an example* *of Chippendale's complete house-furnishing service, which supplied the customer with enormous quantities of furniture of all kinds*

society, and at every level people shamelessly flattered their superiors, seeking their 'protection' in order to become a Member of Parliament, be given a commission in a good regiment, find a relative a job in the customs service, and so on. Similarly, the government of the day used the resources of the state – concessions, offices, sinecures, pensions – as forms of patronage, creating a host of dependants that helped to keep it in power. The entire public domain tended to be viewed by the governing class as legitimate booty, and inconvenient laws were apt to be ignored – although the punishments were savage if the offenders belonged to the lower orders and had infringed the property rights of their betters. In short, British society combined hierarchical structure and ceremonious manners with an outlook that was in many respects venal and self-seeking.

Thomas Chippendale had to make his way in this world, and probably accepted its values. At any rate we should not be surprised if we find him dedicating his book to a belted earl or royal personage, going in for a little smuggling, or taking part in a rigged auction; and it would be a mistake to suppose that any of these activities necessarily harmed his reputation. He was a businessman in a fiercely competitive trade, running a complicated operation from an expensive prime site in London; he had to look out for himself in order to survive, and did so effectively enough, though without, it seems, dying rich.

Chippendale's society also gave him the means to exploit these opportuni-

Right: *A design for brasswork around a keyhole. The* Director *(1762), Pl.CC*

ties. He was born into a vigorous craft tradition that was still capable of further refinement and not yet threatened by factory mass-production. And he came to manhood when heavy furniture was becoming outmoded – a time when creative change was in the air. This was not just a matter of a demand for lighter or more elegant furniture, but involved a simple but decisively important technical change – in broad terms, the replacement of walnut by mahogany as the wood used for quality furniture.

Introduction of mahogany

This began in 1720, when a scarcity of walnut in France, Britain's chief supplier, led to a ban on exports of the wood. As a result, mahogany was brought in to Britain, mainly from the West Indies (in theory from British possessions, but in practice from Cuba as well), and used as a substitute; it was expensive but, as we have seen, there were plenty of Britons who could afford it. The dark reddish hue of mahogany was much to 18th-century tastes, but it was some time before cabinet-makers and their clients realized that the wood had distinctive qualities of its own that could be exploited. Because it was strong, hard and close-grained it could be carved in finer detail than walnut, and its construction could be lighter and more graceful without detriment to its durability. Beginning his career when his principal medium was still fresh, and delightful new styles were taking hold, Chippendale became the first great figure of the Age of Mahogany.

The ensuing chapters of this book describe Chippendale's life, his designs, his furniture, the nature of his business and his relations with his clients. He and his contemporaries are freely quoted, but 18th-century spelling, punctuation and use of capital letters have generally been modernized for the sake of reading comfort; however, quotations are reproduced in their original form where this imparts an interesting or instructive period flavour.

Above: Design for a frame for a marble slab. The Director *(1762), Pl.CLXXVI. Chippendale designed many intricate frames for mirrors and marble slabs*

Right: Mahogany lyre-backed chair by Chippendale, 1768. The chair was made for Stourhead, the Palladian mansion designed by Colen Campbell for the banker, Sir Henry Hoare

Dressing commode, veneered with oriental lacquer and partly japanned. Harewood House

16

Chapter Two

THE YEARS OF OBSCURITY

Chippendale's skills were in part hereditary, for he was born into a family of carpenters and joiners. Nothing is known of his apprentice years, although tradition has associated him early on with two famous Yorkshire houses, Nostell Priory and Harewood House. His first known client of distinction was Richard Boyle, Earl of Burlington, an important patron of the arts, whose custom undoubtedly did much for Chippendale's reputation. By the early 1750s he was clearly doing very well, becoming the owner of an impressive house near the Strand, and later of extensive premises in St Martin's Lane.

Thomas Chippendale has often been called the Shakespeare of English furniture, and like the great dramatist he is a curiously elusive personality. Until recent times so little was known of his life and work that some writers were inclined to minimize his actual achievements, suggesting that he was just an entrepreneur who employed others to design his famous pattern-book and such furniture as could be certainly attributed to the Chippendale firm. Later research has largely discredited this point of view, confirming Chippendale's skill as a designer and identifying many new pieces as his work. But we still know much less about the man Chippendale than we should like, and apart from bills and business letters there are disappointingly few contemporary references to him or his work; despite their habitual interest in

Above: *The tapestry room, Osterley Park, showing scenes taken from* The Loves of the Gods *by François Boucher, signed and dated 1775 by Jacques Neilson, Gobelins. The chairs and sofa were designed by Chippendale c.1770*

the contemporary scene, the gossipy correspondents and writers of diaries and memoirs, normally wonderful sources for the social history of the 18th century, remain silent on the subject of its greatest cabinet-maker.

This is less surprising than it seems. In 18th-century terms Chippendale was never of more than middling status. He was a mere tradesman in a class-conscious society where only distinguished birth, great wealth, or the membership of a few privileged professions (for example the law) gave a man any great consequence. Had Chippendale been a writer or painter, however, he might have received rather more consideration, since the outstanding practitioners of these 'fine arts' were widely recognized as exceptional beings whose doings were worth recording.

But the case was quite different with the 'applied' or 'mechanical' arts. Although the aristocratic patron might have a taste for fine furniture and be discriminating enough to pick the best available cabinet-maker to execute his commissions, he viewed the craftsman himself in much the same light as he viewed his tailor – and took a similarly aloof, leisurely attitude when it came to settling his bills.

Before condemning the 18th century too harshly for its arbitrary values, we should remember that the distinction between fine and applied arts – arts to be appreciated and arts 'only' for use – was several centuries old and was not seriously challenged until late Victorian times; and of course the 20th century has blind spots and prejudices of its own, notably the critical neglect of popular arts such as the cinema until too late to save early material. No doubt later centuries will be just as wise at our expense. However, 20th-century research has at least made generous amends to Thomas Chippendale, with the paradoxical result that today we probably know more about him and his business affairs than anyone in his own time but his family and close associates! A number of traditions, for example that he was a Worcestershire man, have been convincingly refuted, and a thorough analysis of the available material has given us as clear a picture of the man as we are ever likely to get.

A Yorkshire family

Thomas Chippendale was a Yorkshireman, and what we know of his later customers and business contacts suggests that local ties remained important to him throughout his working life. He was born in the little market town of Otley, where he was baptized in June 1718: in the parish register he is recorded as 'Thomas Son of John Chippindale of Otley joyner bap ye 5th'. English spelling had not yet become standardized, and 'Chippindale' remained a common alternative, used on occasion by Thomas himself, to the form handed down to posterity on the title-page of his famous book.

The Chippendales were evidently a sturdy breed of Yorkshire craftsmen, for they had been established in the area around Otley – Wharfedale – for at least ten generations by the time Thomas was born. Both his father and grandfather

were variously described as carpenters or joiners, and other members of the family were similarly employed. 'Joiner' was a more prestigious term than carpenter, implying the possession of special constructive skills – the ability to 'join' separate pieces of wood (for example by using the mortice and tenon principle, or dovetailing) rather than merely to shape single items by sawing, planing or gouging. (A third category, that of cabinet-maker, was becoming established in metropolitan usage from about the time of Chippendale's birth.) However, a craftsman in a

Above: Nostell Priory which was completely furnished by Chippendale's firm, down to the chopping block in the Lower Hall

small local community would normally be prepared to turn his hand to a variety of jobs, and we know that one busy Chippendale, Thomas's cousin William, at various times worked as a carpenter, joiner, timber valuer, builder and surveyor. So it is clear that Thomas Chippendale grew up in a lively, wide-ranging craft tradition in which a variety of skills were passed on from father to son. We can hardly doubt that this was where Thomas acquired his basic skills, though where and when he got his conventional schooling is not known: he was certainly well-equipped for his later business career, being numerate, literate and capable of writing adequately ingratiating and explanatory letters to wealthy and often irate customers.

Beyond this, Chippendale's life is factually a blank for decades – until 1747, when he was almost thirty years old and on the verge of making a success in London. We know nothing of his apprentice years, of how he came to London from a little town off the main coaching routes, or of the conditions or achievements that made his success possible.

Chippendale traditions

There are, however, two traditions worth recording. One says that Chippendale was employed as a joiner at Nostell Priory, where he made the well-known doll's house that is still on the premises. According to other, 'at an early age his genius was recognized by the Lascelles family, of Harewood House, and by the influence of that distinguished family, he, Thomas Chippendale, commenced business in London'. These statements are perfectly plausible, since the houses concerned are in Yorkshire, and in later years Chippendale became responsible for furnishing both of them; his commission for Harewood was actually the most lucrative of his entire career. The link is further strengthened by the fact that Harewood House is a mere eight miles from Chippendale's native Otley, so that in this case it is hardly possible to doubt the existence of some sort of 'Yorkshire connection' favouring Chippendale in later life. However, that does not constitute proof that these stories of early patronage are true, since the 'traditions' emerged when Chippendale's connections with Nostell and Harewood were already known; and some authorities think that they are much too good to be true.

Yet how else than by patronage could Chippendale have reached London, and why should he, with his extensive family connections in Wharfedale, make the long journey to a metropolis where he probably did not have a single friend? In an area rife with speculation, perhaps it is possible to add one more. Thomas Chippendale was an only child whose mother died when he was eleven. His father remarried and had a new family of seven children. Perhaps Thomas, like so many heroes of folk-tales, found himself an outsider – if not actually badly treated – in a house run by a stepmother; and, again like the folk-hero, left for the big city in quest of fame and

Overleaf left: *Exterior of the famous dolls' house at Nostell Priory; attributed to Thomas Chippendale*

Overleaf right: *Interior of the dolls' house which can still be seen at Nostell Priory. The detail of the rooms and furniture is beautifully executed*

Above: Richard Boyle, the third Earl of Burlington, was one of Chippendale's earliest clients. He was a major figure in promoting the graceful 'Palladian' style

fortune. The big city need not in the first instance have been London, since the thriving county town of York might well have provided the kind of experience that Chippendale needed before moving south. Nor does this hypothesis exclude the possibility that he had also secured some degree of help from local notables to make his way in the world.

This was not necessarily a matter of handing out cash; in fact a promise of future custom and some recommendations to friends would have been an effective form of patronage, and of a sort particularly congenial to the 18th-century wielder of influence, since it cost nothing while being productive of a gratifying deference on the part of the recipient.

An early client

It may or may not have been a coincidence that Chippendale's earliest known client, though not a Yorkshireman, held extensive lands in the county. Richard Boyle, Earl of Burlington, was a major figure in the history of English taste, promoting the graceful 'Palladian' style of architecture in the early part of the 18th century. He was an amateur architect of ability (Chiswick House in west London was built to his designs) and the patron of such leading artists as Colen Campbell and William Kent. In a private account book entry dated 13 October 1747, Burlington wrote the maddeningly enigmatic statement 'to Chippendale in full £6.16.0'; nothing is known of the work done by Chippendale, although the surrounding entries in the book make it likely that he had supplied furniture for one of two splendid mansions, Chiswick House or Burlington House (also in London, and remodelled for Burlington some years earlier by Campbell).

The relationship went no further, but since Burlington died in 1753 this may not have any particular significance. The fact that Burlington employed him at all indicates that Chippendale was already an accomplished craftsman, capable of working to the highest metropolitan standards, and acknowledged as such.

Doubtless he was already established in London by this time, although the first direct evidence dates from the following year. In the marriage register of St George's Chapel, Mayfair, the entry for 19 May 1748 records the wedding of 'Thomas Chippendale & Catherine Redshaw, of St Martins-in-the-Fields'. On the face of it St George's Chapel was an odd choice, since it was notorious as a place where instant ceremonies were performed – mainly to accommodate one or more partners too drunk to know better, or to make it possible for an adventurer or adventuress to secure an heiress or heir before the unlucky parents could intervene. (Five years later a Marriage Act would end this situation by making it compulsory to announce a forthcoming wedding – 'put up the banns' – three times before it could take place.) Since nothing is known of Catherine Redshaw it seems unlikely that she was an heiress, though it is still just possible that this was a runaway match. The alternative explanation – that, at a guinea a time, St George's was cheap – would not say much for Chippendale's business prospects in 1748.

However, it is clear that he was already established somewhere in the relatively small part of London just west of Covent Garden, an area that housed most of the capital's better cabinet-makers. Chippendale's first two chil-

Above: *This staircase and hall designed by John Chute for The Vyne, Hampshire, is a good example of the Palladian style of architecture of the eighteenth century*

dren were baptized at St Paul's, Covent Garden, and St Martin's-in-the-Fields, at the bottom of St Martin's Lane. His first London address was Conduit Court, a yard leading off from the south side of Long Acre and, again, not far from St Martin's Lane; Chippendale, now a husband and father, moved in at Christmas 1749. It is usually supposed

that his rented house must have been too small for Chippendale to work on the premises, but the fact that other furniture makers seem to have lived in the Court around the turn of the 18th century suggests that this may have been possible after all. The master craftsman – the man who worked by himself or ran a workshop in which others were employed – generally lived in or very close to his place of business; among other things this enabled him to keep a watchful eye on his stock, and to be on the spot in the case of a fire, a riot, or trouble with the often recalcitrant craft

Above: *Covent Garden in the eighteenth century. It was here in Covent Garden, home also to many other cabinet-makers, that Chippendale first established himself in a workshop*

workmen of the 18th century, who were much more independent-minded than the factory workers of a few generations later. As we shall see, during the more fully documented phase of his life Chippendale himself followed the rule and lived next door to his business premises.

Chippendale cannot have been an employee at this stage of his career: he was rising too rapidly. By June 1752 he had taken an imposing new house in a much more fashionable area just below the Strand and close to the Thames. The new residence – the first house on the right-hand side as you entered Somerset Court – cost Chippendale £27 a year to rent and was rated at £24 (by comparison with £14 for Conduit Court). Behind Chippendale's dwelling lay Northumberland House, the splendid town residence of the Earl of Northumberland, and because of its proximity Somerset Court was sometimes also known as Northumberland Court – circumstances that Chippendale was unashamedly to exploit in the interests of self-advertisement.

In fact it is quite possible that Chippendale moved to a 'good' address with aristocratic associations as part of his preparations for an ambitious publishing venture which needed all the cachet that he could manufacture for it. By 19 March 1753 matters were sufficiently advanced for him to place an extended advertisement in the *London Daily Advertiser* soliciting subscriptions for *The Gentleman and Cabinet-Maker's Director*, 'Being a New Book of Designs of Household Furniture in the GOTHIC, CHINESE and MODERN TASTE, as improved by the politest and most able Artists'. Further advertisements appeared in other journals, promising that the *Director* would appear in the July or August of 1754; in the event, the work was done sooner, and Chippendale's epoch-making book was published in

April 1754. By that time he had taken the other major step in his career, in December 1753 leasing substantial premises in St Martin's Lane and setting up a firm that would carry the Chippendale name there for the next sixty years. But before pursuing Chippendale's career, it is necessary to take a longer look at the *Director*, which was probably the most influential book in the entire history of furniture.

Below: *Design for a table clockcase. The* Director *(1762), Pl.CLXV*

Window cornice and mock festoon curtains in carved and painted pine. Harewood House

Chapter Three

'MOST ELEGANT AND USEFUL DESIGNS'

The Gentleman and Cabinet-Maker's Director was unique among furniture pattern-books in its range, variety and sophistication. The designs encompassed the three main furniture styles of the day — Gothic, Chinese and Modern (Rococo), all of which indulged the contemporary taste for fantasy. A special feature was the variety of designs for chairs, but there was also a wealth of sofas, couches, beds, tables, commodes and case furniture. Designs for candle stands, picture frames, mirrors, chandeliers, fireplaces and wall coverings were also included, making the *Director* a truly comprehensive guide to interior decoration.

THE

GENTLEMAN

AND

CABINET-MAKER's

DIRECTOR.

BEING A LARGE

COLLECTION

OF THE MOST

Elegant and Useful Designs of Houſhold Furniture

IN THE

GOTHIC, CHINESE and MODERN TASTE:

Including a great VARIETY of

BOOK-CASES for LIBRARIES or Private Rooms, COMMODES, LIBRARY and WRITING-TABLES, BUROES, BREAKFAST-TABLES, DRESSING and CHINA-TABLES, CHINA-CASES, HANGING-SHELVES,	TEA-CHESTS, TRAYS, FIRE-SCREENS, CHAIRS, SETTEES, SOPHA'S, BEDS, PRESSES and CLOATHS-CHESTS, PIER-GLASS SCONCES, SLAB FRAMES, BRACKETS, CANDLE-STANDS, CLOCK-CASES, FRETS,

AND OTHER

ORNAMENTS.

TO WHICH IS PREFIXED,

A Short EXPLANATION of the Five ORDERS of ARCHITECTURE, and RULES of PERSPECTIVE;

WITH

Proper DIRECTIONS for executing the moſt difficult Pieces, the Mouldings being exhibited at large, and the Dimenſions of each DESIGN ſpecified:

THE WHOLE COMPREHENDED IN

One Hundred and Sixty COPPER-PLATES, neatly Engraved,

Calculated to improve and refine the preſent TASTE, and ſuited to the Fancy and Circumſtances of Perſons in all Degrees of Life.

Dulcique animos novitate tenebo. OVID.
Ludentis ſpeciem dabit & torquebitur. HOR.

BY

THOMAS CHIPPENDALE,

Of St. MARTIN's-LANE, CABINET-MAKER.

LONDON,

Printed for the AUTHOR, and ſold at his Houſe in St. MARTIN's-LANE. MDCCLIV.
Alſo by T. OSBORNE, Bookſeller, in Gray's-Inn; H. PIERS, Bookſeller, in Holborn; R. SAYER, Print-ſeller, in Fleetſtreet; J. SWAN, near Northumberland-Houſe, in the Strand. At EDINBURGH, by Meſſrs. HAMILTON and BALFOUR: And at DUBLIN, by Mr. JOHN SMITH, on the Blind-Quay.

In publishing *The Gentleman and Cabi-net-Maker's Director* as a substantial folio volume, Chippendale was breaking completely new ground. In previous years a few pamphlets had appeared which carried a limited range of designs that could be used as patterns for making furniture; but Chippendale's work was on a far more imposing and ambitious scale, illustrating and describing pieces of every current type and in all the received styles. In contrast to the paucity of furniture pattern-books, architectural manuals were quite common, and these often included a section on furniture, the reason being that much furniture was designed to resemble architecture, incorporating cornices, pediments and other features taken from the classical repertoire. It therefore appears that furniture was regarded as a subordinate art by both the public and architects, especially those who liked to control the entire layout of their buildings' interiors. So Chippendale, by publishing the *Director*, may have been implicitly asserting the autonomy of the cabinet-maker's craft, though he was careful to acknowledge that it was one of 'the Arts which are either improved or ornamented by architecture'; and he included a reference section with plans of the five classical Orders of architecture, which a cabinet-maker needed to know if he was to execute the details referred to above correctly and with due respect to the classical scheme of proportions.

The measure of Chippendale's success was the wide distribution of the *Director*, whose three editions followed rapidly one after another. The fact that rival cabinet-makers thought it worth imitating was also highly significant. But there was only one *Director*. Chippendale's designs reflected the most sophis-

Above: The title page of The Gentleman and Cabinet-Maker's Director, *probably the most influential book in the history of furniture*

ticated contemporary taste and also helped to diffuse it, so that his book is at once a monument to the man's genius and a historical document of outstanding value, an indispensable guide to English furniture of the mid-18th century, which is still often described – irrespective of the actual maker – as being in the 'Chippendale style'. However, this kind of furniture in fact drew on a number of different styles, as Chippendale himself stated.

Furniture styles

On the title page of the *Director* Chippendale proclaimed that the book consisted of 'a large collection of the most Elegant and Useful Designs of Household Furniture in the Gothic, Chinese and Modern Taste'. These last-named were the three main styles of the period, and their vogue represented a curious episode in the history of British taste, falling between two periods of classicism and reflecting the engagingly refined eccentricity of which 18th-century aesthetics was capable. Despite their apparent diversity, they possessed one feature in common that explains their near-simultaneous popularity: all three were styles in which the most conspicuous element was a strong vein of fantasy.

During the middle years of the century a kind of escapist impulse expressed itself through exoticism in the British decorative arts, although the engrained national sobriety kept it within certain bounds. Hence the Gothic, Chinese and Modern 'tastes' were not of necessity mutually exclusive; each room in a

Above: *Chippendale's design for an elaborate Rococo chimneypiece, featuring classical themes. The* Director *(1762), Pl.CLXXXIV*

31

house might be furnished in a different style, or a single piece of furniture might represent a mixture of styles. A taste for fantasy is rarely purist: that generally comes – as it did in this case – when the inevitable reaction towards rules and restraint sets in.

Rococo

By 'Modern' – always the stylistic term that is quickest to date, – Chippendale and his contemporaries meant what we now call the Rococo, itself a derisory version of the French *rocaille* (rock-work, as in fantasy constructions such as grottoes). The style originated in France early in the 18th century, when there was a reaction against the weighty classicism of the Baroque style; the consequent taste for something lighter and gayer may also have had political undertones, representing an escape from the stifling, self-conscious grandeurs of the Louis XIV period, when the ambitions of the 'Sun King' involved France in a sequence of long and exhausting wars.

As pioneered by designers such as Jean Bérain and Pierre Lepautre, the Rococo was characterized by pale, bright colours and fluent arabesques. In its mature phase, as essentially a style of interior decoration, it consisted of more or less riotous displays of C- and S-scrolls and curves, created from more or less stylized stretches of foliage, flowers, rocks, shells and cascades, and peopled by entertaining, often grotesque, figures of monkeys, birds and human beings. At its best, Rococo design seems spontaneous and unplanned (an illusion, of course), and one of its prime characteristics is its asymmetry – the abandonment of the mirror-image balance given by symmetrical designs in previous styles.

Opposite: *One of a pair of Chippendale carved giltwood casual tables in the Rococo style*

Right: *Designs for cornices for beds or windows, in the Rococo style. The* Director *(1762), Pl.XXXVII*

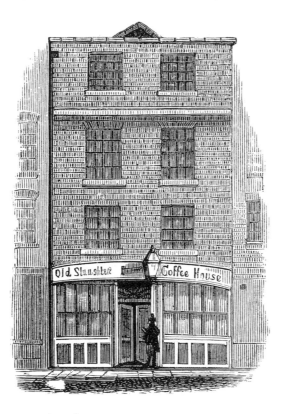

Above: *Slaughter's Coffee House, St Martin's Lane, London, where a group of Rococo enthusiasts met their friends and patrons*

Rococo made little impact in England until the late 1730s, and even then it was mainly taken up by craftsmen such as silversmiths, engravers, porcelain modellers and book illustrators. Only after the death in 1748 of William Kent, the dominant figure in architecture and interior design, was the influence of Rococo felt in those areas – and so little even then that furniture historians have been unable to account for Chippendale's abrupt emergence in the *Director* as a masterly exponent of the style. He may have studied the books of orna-ments that appeared in the middle years of the century, but they had little relevance to furniture except for fixed elements on which the carving could be done without having to take much account of the function to be performed – elements such as mirrors, brackets, picture-frames and console tables (tables placed against the wall and essentially part of its decorative scheme). Where Chippendale found the models and practised the skills needed to apply the Rococo style to chairs and case furniture is not known, although one suggestion is extremely attractive for geographical reasons. Two vitally important centres for the diffusion of Rococo ideas stood in the very street where Chippendale set up in business – the St Martin's Lane Academy and Old Slaughter's Coffee House. Probably inspired by the immigrant French designer Hubert Gravelot, a group of enthusiasts for Rococo taught or studied at the Academy and met their friends and patrons at the Coffee House; and it has been suggested that Chippendale was one of the students.

Powerful objections to the theory – apart from the lack of any concrete evidence to support it! – are that only one member of this entire Rococo circle subscribed to the *Director* (which surely indicates that Chippendale did not belong to it), and that the little we do know about Chippendale's contacts suggests that he mixed with his own class – tradesmen – rather than people from higher social groups such as the Academy students. Yet the evidence of sheer proximity – circumstantial, but extremely persuasive – is hard to set aside. Perhaps Chippendale was at St Martin's but not of it: was the common little man at the back of the room, unregarded but taking a great deal in? Or perhaps the search for inspirations and sources overlooks the extent to which creative talent is capable of absorbing ideas that are 'in the air'.

However he did it, Chippendale somehow took the measure of a style that many craftsmen found particularly difficult just because it could not be reduced to a set of rules or formulas (plenty of bad Rococo design has survived to prove the point). He then successfully adapted it to English tastes, which never took to the extreme forms of Rococo that flourished in France before the style disappeared altogether in the middle years of the 18th century. Chippendale's naturalization of Rococo was an important achievement, without which the *Director* could never have achieved the influence it did.

Chinoiserie

The 'Chinese taste' was in a sense a revival, for Chinese lacquered furniture and other goods had appeared in Europe during the 17th century and had given rise to imitations even then. 'Imitations' is not in fact the appropriate word, since Europeans were not intent upon reproducing authentic Chinese wares but on giving a 'Chinese' character to their interiors, furniture, porcelain and gardens. This 'Chinese' character was partly derived from a misunderstanding of Chinese culture, but mainly reflected a conscious delight in manipulating fantasy images of the

Right: *This design for a Chinese Chippendale bed is typical of the revival in interest in* chinoiserie, *begun during the seventeenth century. The* Director *(1762), Pl.XXXII*

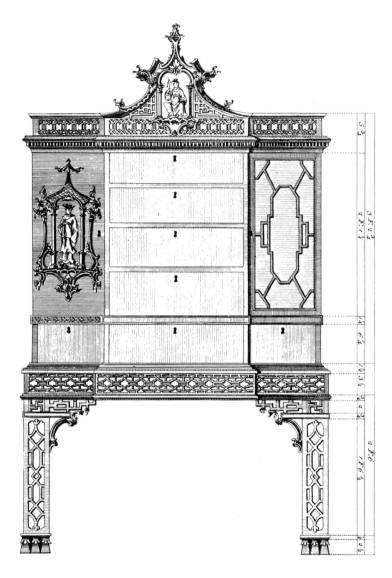

Orient − pagodas, dragons, men with coolie-hats and drooping moustaches, dream landscapes and so on.

The received term for this Euro-Chinese style is *chinoiserie*. In its earliest English phase it mainly took the form of designs applied to the surfaces of standard furniture types; the technique used was japanning, a form of varnishing developed to imitate Oriental lacquer, a thick, tough, brilliant resin coating which could be stained, painted, carved or inlaid. Japanning was to remain one of the outstanding features of *chinoiserie*, but when the real vogue of the movement began in the 1740s, entire rooms, including wallpapers and hangings, were furnished according to the Chinese taste, and the actual shape and construction of furniture were modified accordingly. By 1753 a contributor to the *World* could claim that:

> *According to the present prevailing whim, everything is Chinese, or in the Chinese taste; or, as it is sometimes more modestly expressed, **partly after the Chinese manner**. Chairs, tables, chimney-pieces, frames for looking-glasses, and even our most vulgar utensils are all reduced to this new-fangled standard; and without doors so universally has it spread, that every gate to a cow-yard is in Ts and Zs, and every hovel for the cows has bells hanging at the corners.*

In other words *chinoiserie* had become a positive craze, spreading to private houses and also to public places such as the Vauxhall pleasure gardens. Persons

Above: *This design for a Chinese cabinet is an example of the vogue for chinoiserie. The* Director *(1762), Pl.CXXIII*

Opposite: *Chinese Chippendale fourposter with elaborate canopy and cream silk curtains, Victoria and Albert Museum*

Above: *Design for a china case which exemplifies Chinese Chippendale with its geometrical fretwork, lattice-work and pagoda roofs. The* Director *(1762), Pl.CXXXV*

with classical tastes were inclined to look down on it (as they looked down on Rococo), and as early as 1749 Mrs Elizabeth Montagu outdid the *World* in her disdainful comments on the new trend: 'Thus has it happened in furniture . . . we must all seek the barbarous gaudy *goût* of the Chinese; and fat-headed Pagods and shaking Mandarins bear the prize from the finest works of antiquity; and Apollo and Venus must give way to a fat idol with a sconce on his head.' Mrs Montagu was a leading 'bluestocking', as intellectual and literary women were called in that period; but she nonetheless found fashion irresistible, and three years later made an implicit but outright retraction by installing a 'Chinese' room in her own house. Ironically, the surviving cabinet and writing-desk made for this scorner of *chinoiserie* are of considerable historical interest, being the earliest datable examples of furniture made (as opposed to merely decorated) in the Chinese taste.

It therefore appears that *chinoiserie* was well established as a furniture style before Chippendale published the *Director*, and Chippendale's own notes on the plates imply that he himself had already made and sold a good many of the pieces illustrated. The loss of so much early *chinoiserie* furniture makes it difficult to be sure quite how original Chippendale was, but when compared with the patterns issued by previous designers, the *Director* can certainly be described as incomparably richer in decorative resources as well as more wide-ranging in applying the style to various types of furniture. Chippendale was obviously proud of this aspect of his work, making free with adjectives such as 'magnificent' and throwing out such remarks as 'there has been none like them yet made'. And indeed 'Chinese Chippendale', with its geometrical fretwork and lattice-work, its pagoda roofs and its wealth of mock-Chinese figures, flowers and birds, constitutes one of his great achievements, exhibiting a playful distinction of its own that remains in close sympathy with Rococo.

Below: *This china case is again in the Chinese style, a style that was well established before Chippendale wrote the* Director. The Director *(1762),* Pl.CXXXVII

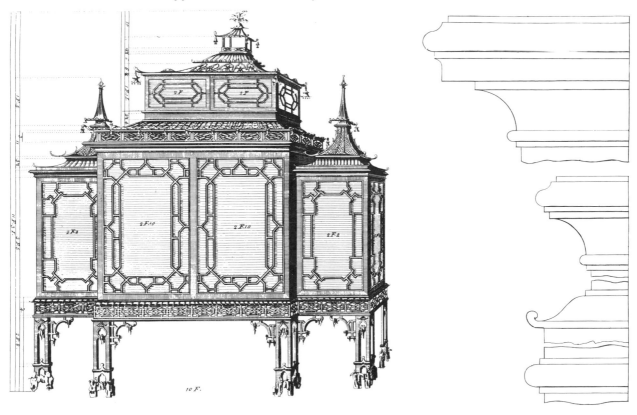

Gothic

The third *Director* style, Gothic, was also fanciful and anti-classical, but was derived from the native tradition. Gothic was the architectural style of the High Middle Ages, most simply identified by its employment of pointed arches; in England, unlike the Continent, it had never been entirely abandoned as a suitable style for ecclesiastical buildings, despite the denigration implied in its name. The Goths were a barbarian people who played a significant role in the destruction of the Roman Empire, and 'Gothic' was coined in the 17th century as a term of abuse directed at the medieval style, which was taken to symbolize an age of darkness and superstition. The 18th-century attitude was not materially different, except that sophisticates like Horace Walpole now found a certain charm in 'venerable barbarism', and felt thrilled by the idea of 'imprinting the gloomth of abbeys and cathedrals on one's house'.

Walpole was in fact the chief creator of the vogue for the Gothic. The style had been employed occasionally in the 1740s, spurred on by the publication of Batty and Thomas Langley's *Ancient Architecture* (1742), with its 'great variety of grand and useful designs, entirely new, in the Gothic mode, for the ornamenting of buildings and gardens'.

Opposite: Gothic, the third style in Chippendale's Director, *was fanciful and anti-classical. The Great Hall at Strawberry Hill is typical of this style*

But it was Walpole, man of letters and antiquarian connoisseur, who built the famous Strawberry Hill, a small Gothic house at Twickenham, filled with stained glass and old furniture, which deeply impressed his contemporaries as it took shape in the early 1750s. Although informed by a genuine antiquarian spirit, Strawberry Hill was Gothic on an inappropriately small scale, and adapted to take in the home comforts that were a necessity to Walpole; and during the subsequent fashion for Gothic, designers paid even less attention to authenticity, manipulating decorative details at will and combining them with elements taken from other styles.

Influence of the Gothic novel

By 1753, when Chippendale must have been working on the *Director*, the *World* believed that 'the last fashion, the Gothic' was fast giving way to *chinoiserie*, although shortly before 'our home, our beds, our bookcases and our couches were all copied from some parts or other of our old cathedrals'. However, the Gothic refused to die, and in 1764 it received a fresh impetus from the publication of Walpole's novel *The Castle of Otranto*. This pioneered a new literary genre, the Gothic novel, the 18th-century equivalent of the horror story, replete with furious baronial and monkish passions, feuds, dungeons, secret crimes, and forays into the sensational, superstitious and supernatural. In architecture and the decorative arts the Gothic remained a minority taste, but one sufficiently persistent to justify

Above: *The Gothic style was considered particularly suitable for the library. This bookcase is a good example. The* Director *(1762), Pl.XII*

Chippendale in keeping Gothic designs in later editions of the *Director*.

Gothic furniture was made for most purposes, but it was felt to be especially appropriate for the library. No doubt this was because learning had for centuries been the province of the medieval Church, so that study was still charged with 'monastic' associations. Features of the Gothic style employed by Chippendale in *Director* furniture include pointed arches, usually in the form of the double-curved, flame-like ogee arch; delicate fretwork fashioned to resemble the cusped (pointed) tracery that was, for example, employed on Gothic windows; and projecting pinnacles with regular leaf decorations (crockets) and topped with a fleur-de-lys ornament (finial). Although it might have a look of massive seriousness when used in a library, Gothic too could be

Above: Two Rococo chair designs, showing possible variations of style in the front legs and feet. The Director (1762), Pl.XII

combined with elements of the other *Director* styles, all three of which lent themselves to virtuoso treatment by the cabinet-maker.

Chair designs

Chippendale set up his shop in St Martin's Lane 'at the sign of the Chair', and the 'Chippendale chair' is still the most famous of all his creations. It would really be more accurate to speak of 'the Chippendale chairs', for the *Director* offers an impressive variety of designs for this one item of furniture –

38 in the first edition (14 plates), raised to 60 (25 plates) in the third edition of 1762.

Easily the largest group consisted of chairs in the Rococo style. These were exemplified by what Chippendale called his 'new pattern' chairs – a dozen-strong basic collection of pieces with

Above: One of eight Chippendale arm-chairs, ordered for the library of Harewood House. This armchair was originally japanned blue and upholstered in yellow

open rectangular backs whose solid construction can easily be overlooked in the contemplation of their decorative qualities.

Decorations

Characteristic features include an undulating, serpentine or cupid's-bow top rail; a splat (central upright on the back) pierced and carved in elaborate but elegant low-relief patterns; uprights on each side of the back that curve gently upwards and outwards; and cabriole or straight front legs. The cabriole leg curved outwards from the seat rail to form a 'knee' before curving inwards and tapering down to the foot of the chair. It had been popular for decades, mainly in conjunction with the claw and ball foot (which is exactly what its name suggests – a foot shaped like a ball held by the claw of a real or imagined animal). But Chippendale dispensed with this kind of foot completely in the

Above right: *Ribband back mahogany armchair showing rich carving on the legs*

Above left: *Ribband back chair in which the splat is transformed into a profusion of knotted ribbons. The Director (1762), Pl.XV*

Director, though it is not clear whether he omitted it because he sensed that it was about to go out of fashion, or caused it to go out of fashion by omitting it. Instead he mainly showed scroll feet, which might either turn outwards (French scrolls) or inwards (knurl feet).

Straight legs had only come back into fashion around 1750, and one of the odder features of this development was that stretchers came back with them. Stretchers were the horizontal bars under a chair that connected the legs; they were added in order to reinforce the structure, a rational proceeding

when the wood used was a soft one. But when the chair was made of mahogany, stretchers were unnecessary; so it seems that they reappeared simply because they had previously 'belonged' with straight legs.

Above left: *One of a pair of red lacquer Chinese chairs. The style suggests lightness and delicacy and was considered suitable for a lady's dressing room*

Above right: *A Chinese Chippendale armchair showing characteristic lattice-work in the back, and straight legs*

Ribband back chairs

Chippendale's most extravagant, luxurious Rococo pieces were the 'ribband back' chairs, in which the splat was transformed into a profusion of knotted and interlaced ribbons which trailed from side to side as well as from top to bottom, linking the uprights as well as the top rail and the seat. The legs and seat rail were also richly carved. Chippendale was immensely proud of these chairs, claiming that they were 'if I may speak without vanity . . . the best I have ever seen (or perhaps have ever been made)', and that one he had made 'had an excellent effect, and gave satisfaction to all who saw it'. Although the ribband-back chairs might be thought to have appealed only to clients with markedly 'French' tastes and very well-lined pockets, Chippendale stated in the third edition of the *Director* (1762) that 'Several sets have been made, which have given entire satisfaction'. However, it is perhaps significant that he added, 'If any of the small ornaments should be thought superfluous, they may be left out, without spoiling the design.' Clients were recommended to cover the seats with red Morocco.

French chairs

The *Director* also included what Chippendale termed 'French Chairs', upholstered armchairs with curling and returning scrollwork frames, open arms and an open space between the back and the seat rail. By contrast, his 'Chinese' chairs emphasized straight lines and geometrical forms, although the effect was sometimes modified by ornaments that broke the line of the top rail; and on

one occasion Chippendale could not resist the temptation to crown a chair with a pagoda crest. The backs were filled with lattice-work in patterns that are sometimes pleasing and curiously modern in their geometry; but others, inevitably, now seem over-elaborate and Chinese-puzzle-like. All the chairs had straight legs connected by stretchers. The legs, the stretchers, and the brackets inserted at the junction of the leg and seat, might all be fretted, and the combination of lattice-work and fretting gave 'Chinese Chippendale' chairs their lightness and delicacy. In a comment that illuminates the varied

Below: *Designs for Chinese chairs emphasizing straight lines and geometric forms. The* Director *(1762), Pl.XXVII*

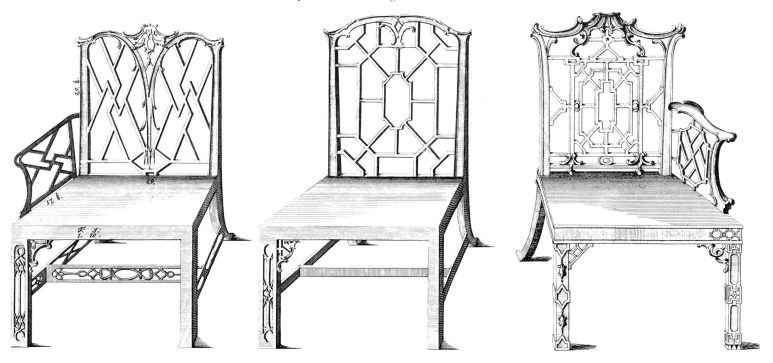

settings of elegant 18th-century social life, Chippendale remarked that such chairs were 'very popular for a lady's dressing-room: especially if it is hung with India paper. They will likewise suit Chinese temples. They have commonly cane bottoms, with loose cushions.'

The Gothic style was applied less successfully to chairs, offering little more than an alternative decorative repertoire with which to vary the patterns of chair-backs. Moreover Chippendale's Gothic designs for hall chairs are eccentric in a rather forbidding way and, not surprisingly, seem to have exercised little influence on contemporary taste.

Above: A traditional Chippendale mahogany carved settee that would generally be placed in a hall

Opposite: A highly elaborate Rococo design for a state bed. No effort is spared in suggesting luxury and magnificence. The Director (1762), Pl.XLVII

Sofas

The remaining seat furniture in the *Director* consisted of sofas and couches, of conventional design except for two extravagant 'Chinese Sophas' equipped with draped pagoda-like canopies. This

49

Above left: Mahogany and rosewood Pembroke table at Nostell Priory. A rosewood drawer is for backgammon and the underside is set out as a chessboard

Above right: Artist's table with a hinged top. Nostell Priory 1767

was followed by a section on beds – Rococo beds, dome beds, Gothic beds, couch beds, Chinese beds, state beds, field beds – which represented the height of luxury, smothering the four-poster structures in lavish ornament and gorgeous drapes.

Tables

Chippendale illustrated an even greater variety of tables. The rectangular-topped side table (he called it a 'sideboard table') might be extremely plain, with a mere hint of *chinoiserie* in the small fretted brackets at the angles between legs and top, or might aspire to a 'French' opulence of decoration. Writing tables were either rectangular and flat-surfaced, with drawers immediately beneath, or of the familiar type with a superstructure of little drawers and pigeon-holes at the back. 'Bureau tables', which Chippendale later preferred to call 'bureau dressing tables', were bedroom pieces with sets of drawers and a kneehole, by no means as ornate as the 'lady's dressing table', complete with a 'dressing-glass' on folding hinges and gilt ornaments. Breakfast tables were also much used in the bedroom by the leisured classes; they were equipped with let-down flaps on either side so that they could be quickly and easily removed. *Chinoiserie* fretwork could be used on breakfast tables (and was doubtless *de rigueur* for the Chinese bedroom), and also on the little railings or galleries round the tops of 'China tables', pleasing little tables that held the tea-things all fashionable people possessed; since these were made of valuable porcelain, the railings were functional as well as decorative features.

For some reason none of the editions of the *Director* includes a design for a dining table. Admittedly this piece of furniture had come down in the world and was no longer a grand fixture as it had been in the 17th century. In Chippendale's day people preferred to use several smaller tables with drop-leaves which could be raised by gate legs that swung out and under them. When not in use, these could be banished to a corridor, while on very formal occasions at which large numbers of people had to be seated together, the tables could be united with stirrup clips and covered with a large cloth. But although Chippendale included some very basic designs in the *Director* for the benefit of

Above: *Design for a clock case. The* Director *(1762), Pl.CLXIV*

crowning arches. It seems unlikely that such pieces were made without serious modifications, and Chippendale implicitly admitted as much when he wrote of one design that it would give him 'great pleasure to see it executed, as I doubt not of its making an exceeding genteel and grand appearance'.

Chinese style

The Chinese style was strongly favoured for shelves, cases and cabinets – appropriately so, since they were often used for displaying china and other exotic objects. One cabinet is described as

Above: Pair of broken pedimented Chippendale bookcases c.1760

'the richest and most magnificent . . . perhaps in all Europe'; however, this was evidently another instance of a design of such intricacy that it was never realized, for Chippendale also remarks that 'I had a particular pleasure in retouching and finishing this design, but should have much more in the execution of it, as I am confident I can make the work more beautiful and striking than the drawing' – an interesting personal note and a rather touching implicit appeal to some hoped-for patron of wealth and discernment.

Carver's pieces

The *Director* carried a range of designs for other types of case furniture, including chests of drawers, clothes presses (wardrobes), examples of the combined 'desk and bookcase' (bureau bookcase), and clock cases. In a very different category are Chippendale's much admired designs for 'carvers' pieces' (that is, pieces in which the skill lies in the carving, not in the cabinet-work). These included candle stands (also called *torchères*), picture frames, and above all the frames for mirrors of various kinds. Mirror glass was extremely expensive, so it was an ideal subject for conspicuous consumption, especially in the case of pier glasses and girandoles; the pier glass was a tall wall mirror, the girandole a small wall mirror with a bracket in which to hold a candle. On all these luxury pieces the decoration ran riot (especially in the third edition), mixing Rococo at its most excessive with touches of the classical and the Chinese; lodged here and there among the all-encompassing waves of scrollwork and sprouting foliage we can spot fantastic long-beaked birds, putti (cupids), Chinese figures with coolie-hats, ruins, trophies (neatly composed, quasi-heraldic groups of arms and armour or musical instruments), urns, etc.

These pieces were obviously popular, since they figured even more prominently in the enlarged third edition of 1762. This demonstrated in the most material fashion that the *Director* had satisfied a real need, since the designs in it were more wide-ranging as well as more numerous than before. New items included profusely decorated chimney-pieces, 'lanthorns' (lanterns) and chandeliers, as well as humble basin stands, a shaving table and stove grates. Within the covers of a single publication the reader could now find designs for 'chamber organs', borders for damask and paper hangings, and a variety of pieces that included some very eccentric garden seats, 'terms for busto's' (tall stands for busts), pedestals and cisterns for cooling wine. Patently the intention, carried out with complete success, was to make the *Director* the indispensable pattern-book for an entire generation of clients and craftsmen.

Below: *Design for a stove grate. The* Director *(1762), Pl.CXCI*

The Adam saloon at Nostell Priory. Furniture by Haig and Chippendale, c.1780

56

Chapter Four

CHIPPENDALE OF ST MARTIN'S LANE

In partnership with James Rannie, Chippendale occupied extensive premises in St Martin's Lane. Despite a fire in 1755 business went from strength to strength. Rannie's death in 1766 imposed considerable strains, but Chippendale remained in charge of the craft and design side of the firm, enjoying the patronage of such distinguished clients as David Garrick, the Duke of Atholl and Viscount Melbourne, and working with the greatest architects of the day – Sir William Chambers, James Wyatt and Robert Adam.

the *Director* was to remedy his lack of London contacts, but if so he was taking a great risk, since the success of the book could not have been a foregone conclusion unless the author's qualities were already known. Nor would he have been able to persuade a successful Scottish businessman to become his partner in a potentially expensive venture on the uncertain basis of a book published by an unknown author. It seems impossible to resist the conclusion that some powerful influence, whether reputation, money or contacts, was operating in Chippendale's favour during this period, giving him the confidence to make a strong bid for eminence.

Early years in business

The partner in question was an upholsterer and cabinet-maker named James Rannie, who was installed in St Martin's Lane by August 1754; he was a man of substance who may well have contributed the lion's share of the capital and managed the business side of the partnership. The premises consisted of three houses, numbers 60, 61 and 62 St Martin's Lane; Chippendale lived at no. 60, no. 61 was the shop – The Cabinet and Upholstery Warehouse at the sign of the chair – and Rannie dwelt at no. 62. How much Chippendale had come up in the world can be gauged by the fact that the property was rated at £124, almost five times the rating of his Northumberland Court house. His firm was ideally situated opposite Slaughter's Coffee House, whose cultivated clientele were almost certain to notice the sign of the

Taken together, Chippendale's new premises and the almost simultaneous publication of his book represent an ambitious new departure for an apparently obscure designer-craftsman. The qualification implied in the word 'apparent' is surely justified: it is difficult to believe that Chippendale would have taken the financial risks that must have been involved in this double venture unless he already had a substantial reputation or an assured clientele, despite the admitted lack of evidence that either ever existed. It has been argued that Chippendale's object in publishing

chair as they came and went. As we have already noted, St Martin's Lane was an important artistic and cultural centre, housing the St Martin's Lane Academy as well as Slaughter's, and attracting successful painters, sculptors and architects to its residential west side. Above all, in St Martin's Lane Thomas Chippendale was close to, and in direct rivalry with, the leading cabinet-makers of the realm.

Chippendale certainly made every effort to benefit as a business proprietor from the publication and subsequent popularity of the *Director*. The announcements of the *Director*'s publication ended: 'N.B. All Sorts of Cabinet and Upholstery Work made by the Author in the neatest and most fashionable Taste, and at the most reasonable Rates.' And, in the preface, Chippendale used the aspersions said to have been cast on his designs as an opportunity to advertise:

I have here given no Design but what may be executed with Advantage by the Hands of a skilful Workman, though some of the Profession have been diligent enough to represent them (especially those after the Gothick and Chinese Manner) as so many specious Drawings . . . I am confident I can convince all Noblemen, Gentlemen, or

Left: *A Chippendale armchair in the Gothic style*

Right: *Copy of Thomas Chippendale's fire insurance policy*

others, who will honour me with their Commands, that every Design in the Book can be improved, both as to Beauty and Enrichment, in the Execution of it, by Their Most Obedient Servant, THOMAS CHIPPENDALE.

Buoyed up by the success of the *Director*, and perhaps by Rannie's capital, Chippendale adapted the St Martin's Lane premises to his requirements. He was evidently still doing so on 4 February 1755, when he took out fire cover with the Sun Insurance Office, since the policy includes £250 on 'a warehouse only intended to be built at the End of the yard'. The actual document has survived, and tells us that the buildings and their contents – household goods, stock in trade and wearing apparel – were insured for a total of £3,700 on payment of an £8.9s premium.

Below: A pair of Chinese Chippendale chairs, c.1770

St Martin's Lane

The action was singularly (some might even think suspiciously) well timed, since there was a fire at the premises just two months later, on 5 April 1755. The *Public Advertiser* describes the event in a splendidly breathless prose made even more urgent and exclamatory by the liberal 18th-century use of capitals:

On Saturday Night a dreadful Fire broke out in the Workshop of Mr Chippendale, in a court in St Martin's Lane, which in its Beginning, the Wind being very high, and a great Scarcity of Water, raged very furiously, and as there was a great

Quantity of Timber on the Premises and that inclosed by Wooden Workshops and Sheds, it threaten'd Destruction to the Neighbourhood of New Street, St Martin's Lane, and even Long-acre.

Presenting an interesting glimpse of mid-Georgian city life, the *Advertiser* goes on to state that fortunately 'by the timely Assistance of the Guards and the Peace Officers, the useless part of the Mob was beat off', and as a result 'the Flames were subdued in much less Time than could have been hoped for in such a tempestuous Night'.

The damage to the premises was moderately serious, being valued by the insurers (whose estimates, to put it mildly, rarely err on the side of generosity) at £847 12s 6d. However, the Sun Office paid up with commendable promptness, and apart from any interruption of business caused by reorganizing and rebuilding, Chippendale and Rannie's losses were probably light.

Chippendale's workmen

The main sufferers appear to have been the firm's journeymen (skilled workmen), for twenty-two boxes of their tools perished in the fire, and in the pre-factory era workmen were expected to supply their own equipment. Since they were not insured, this meant the loss of their livelihood unless charitable people came to the rescue. The men immediately set up their own fund, putting notices in the *Public Advertiser* appealing for contributions, which by June were said to have amounted to a quarter of the

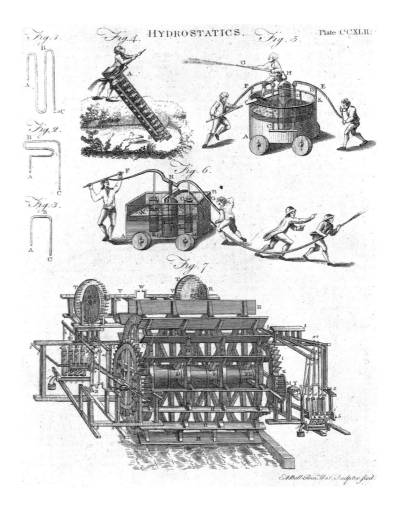

Above: *Methods of firefighting in the eighteenth century. Thomas Chippendale's own workshop was badly damaged by fire*

sum needed. It would be interesting to know how Chippendale reacted (did he help his old employees, or did he simply lay them off and take on a new workforce?), but there is no record of this or of the fate of the unlucky journeymen. The incident does have an advantage from our point of view, in that it fixes the minimum number of workmen employed by Chippendale in

Above: *Chinese Chippendale settee from Claydon House, Buckinghamshire*

to more than one interpretation, and are based on mistaken notions of 18th-century ethics. Only very grand people were above the scramble for patronage and spoils, and even if it were true that Chippendale had tried to acquire patronage above his station by a *fait accompli*, it would probably not have been held against him (except, perhaps, by his competitors).

The final version

In what appears to be Chippendale's final version of the *Director*, ninety-four plates were retained from the first and second editions, and 106 new ones were added. The book remained on sale until at least 1766, and was even published in a French edition; Louis XV of France and Catherine the Great of Russia almost certainly owned copies. After that, both Chippendale and his competitors seem to have felt that the market was saturated, for no new furniture pattern-books appeared until some years after Chippendale's death.

Despite various slips and inconsistencies, the third edition of the *Director* has the air of a successful publication, issued by a man who no longer needs to assert his importance so strenuously. Chippendale's preface was shorn of its pretentious classical tags and allusions; he omitted his lengthy disquisition on the artist's failure to live up to his original conception; and enthusiastic self-praise largely disappeared from the notes, although Chippendale did permit himself the occasional dropping of names, as in his description of 'A bed which has been made for the Earls of Dumfries and Morton'. Moreover the original list of subscribers was not reprinted, a decision which suggests that the *Director*'s reputation, like its author's, was too secure to need puffing.

Changes in the 3rd edition

The content of the book also underwent changes in the third edition, as Chippendale intimated on the title page by dropping the earlier reference to 'the Gothic, Chinese and Modern Taste' in favour of the less commital 'In the most Fashionable Taste'. In the plates the difference was not at once apparent, since Chippendale's liking for Rococo and *chinoiserie* remained as strong as ever, and even Gothic, though less well represented than in 1754, was much in evidence. But here and there a new classicizing impulse could be felt, indicating that Chippendale had already sensed that a major change of style was impending. The full development of the style – Neo-Classicism – is the subject

Above: *An opulent tulipwood barometer case, with carved gilt ornament. The barometer was by the Swiss maker Justin Vulliamy. Nostell Priory*

of the next chapter; the third edition of the *Director* was a premonition rather than a true example of it. Chippendale expressed his sense of the new impulse mainly by including individual classical details – putti, trophies, urns, dolphins, rams' heads, ruins, emblems (symbolic devices) and so on – in designs that retained a strongly Rococo or Rococo–Chinese character, much more frivolous and exuberant in mood than Neo-Classical. In fact the designs tended to be more extravagant than ever, especially in the almost entirely new series of carvers' pieces.

New designs

Another striking feature of the third edition was the number of new types of furniture illustrated in it; as pointed out in Chapter 3, these ranged from basin stands and tea-kettles to garden furniture and organs. Combined with helpful remarks on upholstery, decoration and other subjects, the *Director*'s breadth of treatment gave it an encyclopaedic aspect that must have greatly enhanced its authority. And, as we shall see (Chapter 6), this was itself only a reflection of the kind of commissions undertaken by Chippendale and Rannie.

Clients and cash-flow crises

Meanwhile Chippendale's day-to-day business was, we must suppose, flourishing. However, no records of actual work done by Chippendale him-

Below: Top view of the luxurious Diana and Minerva dressing commode, with 'exceeding fine Antique Ornaments', comprising marquetry of various woods with ivory on a satinwood ground. Harewood House. Chippendale regarded this as his finest piece

self or by the firm exist before the year 1757 – a powerful argument in support of those who believe that the publication of the *Director* 'made' Chippendale, although that is not the view put forward in this book. One such transaction involved Arniston House, the Scottish residence of Robert Dundas, Lord Arniston. On 2 April 1757, according to Arniston's household accounts, Chippendale was paid £2 6s for providing a china shelf and a cheese box – not a very momentous event, although there is a strong suspicion that Chippendale carried out other commissions for Arniston House, more particularly a rosewood table now in the Lady Lever Art Gallery at Port Sunlight.

It was also in April 1757 that Chippendale began his much longer connection with Sir John Filmer of East Sutton Park in Kent, which is briefly recorded in the baronet's own account book. Over a period of sixteen years Chippendale performed his usual wide range of services, supplying furniture and fabrics (even two pairs of 'common blankets', for which the charge was £1 6s) as well as five pieces of something called 'Stuccow Paper' at 3s 6d each. Interestingly enough, Filmer's final payment, £379 for 'Furniture etc to the Bow Chamber' of East Sutton, amounted to more than he had spent on Chippendale's work over the previous sixteen years.

From this point onwards, records of the firm's activities, including bills sent in by Chippendale, become relatively abundant; and there are also two invaluable collections of business letters writ-

Above: *Detail from the front of the Diana and Minerva commode at Harewood House – so called because of the figures of the two goddesses executed in marquetry medallions of wood and ivory on the doors*

ten by the cabinet-maker himself. Thanks to these sources it will be possible to describe some of Chippendale's most interesting relationships with his clients (Chapter 6).

Apart from these, nothing of significance is known about Chippendale's activities until 1760, when six plates by him – versions of designs he had used elsewhere – appeared in a book entitled *Household Furniture in Genteel Taste for the Year 1760*. It was an unimpressive production, largely made up of rehashed designs like those by Chippendale, and it can only have run to four editions because it was cheap (initially 7s 3d). Chippendale presumably contributed in order to make a little money or to oblige the publisher, Robert Sayer.

In 1760 Chippendale was also elected to membership of the Society of Arts, an institution intended to promote improvements in design. Membership was unrestricted, so this event tells us nothing about Chippendale's standing other than his willingness to pay two guineas a year for the privilege; in return he may have hoped to make useful contacts among the wealthier members. Either his expectations were disappointed or the difficult circumstances in 1766 caused him to let his membership lapse.

Death of Rannie

The difficulties arose from the death of Chippendale's partner, James Rannie. In consequence an announcement in the *Public Advertiser* of 10 February 1766 informed the public that the partnership was dissolved, and that all claims and payments up to 20 January (presumably the date of Rannie's death) should be settled with the firm's Scottish bookkeeper, Thomas Haig. Haig was very much Rannie's man, and had been appointed as one of his executors, so he was well placed to sort out the finances of the partnership. The executors quickly decided to sell off all the joint stock, and advertised accordingly. The auction notice therefore tells us quite a lot about the materials ready to hand and the goods kept in stock without being made for specific customers:

> a great Variety of fine Mahogany and Tulup Wood, Cabinets, Desks, and Book-Cases, Cloathes Presses, double Chests of Drawers, Commodes, Buroes, fine Library, Writing, Card, Dining, and other Tables, Turky and other Carpets, one of which is 13 Feet by 19 Feet six, fine Pattern chairs, and sundry other Pieces of curious Cabinet Work, a large Parcel of fine season'd Feathers; as also all the large unwrought Stock, consisting of fine Mahogany and other Woods, in Plank, Boards, Vanier [Veneer], and Wainscot.

In the event, the auction that took place seems to have been on a much smaller scale, probably in order to keep Chippendale solvent. Despite notices that 'the Trade will for the future be carried on by Mr Chippendale on his own account', it seems unlikely that he could have done so with a completely empty warehouse and while repaying Rannie's investment in other aspects of the business. The executors evidently decided that it would be stupid to ruin a thriving enterprise which could eventually pay them in full, and it was arranged for Chippendale to carry on.

Above: The library writing table at Nostell Priory, one of Chippendale's finest pieces, with a portrait of Sir Rowland Winn and his wife, the owners of Nostell Priory

This interpretation of events is supported by much circumstantial evidence, and it is not too fanciful to picture the next few years as troubled ones, with Chippendale struggling to pay off a large debt on which interest was rapidly accumulating. In his earliest surviving letter (27 December 1767) he asks his client, Sir Rowland Winn, to assist him with a little money (that is, pay part of his bill) 'as I am in great need at present on account of the death of my late partner, his effects being taken out of trade'. In March 1769 he requested a note for £200, assuring his patron that 'I would not ask any such things if I was not absolutely obliged to make up £500 this week to pay the executors of Mr Rannie my late partner'.

Sir Rowland Winn

Finally, on 20 November 1770, Chippendale wrote to Winn excusing himself for delays in executing the baronet's commissions. He confessed apologetically that 'I have been obliged to do business for ready money only in order to support myself in the best manner I could, and that but very poorly'. The reason was that, after Rannie's death, 'I had but very little money to begin the work again . . . I have since that time made a tolerable shift till this last summer, which has been very fatal to me. I could hardly keep myself out of jail though I have money enough to pay everyone their just debts and as much [as] I want besides for myself, but it was out of my hands.'

This is a graphic, if not very clearly expressed, account of Chippendale's situation, and carries conviction. The final sentence probably means that he 'had money enough' in the sense that he *would have had enough* if it had been in his hands – in other words, if his clients had paid up. This was probably the truth, since it is known that in February 1771 Edwin Lascelles of Harewood House owed Chippendale so much that the cabinet-maker refused to go on with the work he had been commissioned to do – a fairly extreme decision in view of the 18th-century craftsman's dependence on his client's patronage and 'good word'.

In all the letters quoted above, Chippendale was admittedly making strenuous attempts to get a bill paid or excuse his failure to execute orders on time; but although he may have exaggerated the situation he is hardly likely to have invented it. Moreover in April 1771, only a few months after his desperate-sounding letter to Sir Rowland Winn, Chippendale wrote again, but this time as the representative of Chippendale, Haig & Co., and using 'we' to describe the firm's doings. Thomas Haig and another executor of Rannie's will, Henry Ferguson, had gone into partnership with Chippendale, presumably realizing that this was a more satisfactory way of profiting from his ability than keeping him debt-ridden; Haig, Rannie's former book-keeper, may well have borrowed the capital he needed from the widow of his 'late esteemed master'. Although the note of urgency is still heard in Chippendale's later letters (and in January 1772 he again predicted that he would be 'utterly ruined' unless Winn started paying up), they give the impression that the worst was over.

Chippendale remained in charge of the craft and design side of the firm's activities, leaving the business management to Haig; the third man, Ferguson, appears to have been a sleeping partner who preserved his anonymity as the '& Co.' in the firm's title. Consequently Haig stayed in London to watch over affairs while Chippendale, as before, travelled about the country for consultations with clients.

Opposite: *The magnificent Chippendale medal cabinet, with curved facade and decorated top, built in 1767 into a blind door recess in the library at Nostell Priory*

Brushes with the law

He also spent some time in France, which he mentions having recently visited in a letter written to Sir Rowland Winn in October 1768. French furniture was luxurious and enormously prestigious, so on that occasion Chippendale may have gone to buy some pieces for his firm's stock, or to execute one of his client's orders. Or he may have been engaged in a mildly nefarious activity of the sort that misfired on another trip in November the following year. This was to bring in quality chairs from France but greatly undervalue them when making the required declaration to British customs, the point being that the import duties to be paid would be equivalently low. A common device was to dismantle the frames (which could easily be reassembled by any competent craftsman) and pass off the chaotic heap of timbers as 'lumber'.

Chippendale appears to have attempted a more straightforward deceit; according to the official account he 'Entered on board the Calais Packet, John Gilbey from Calais, one Case containing five Dozen of Chairs, unfinished Value Eighteen pounds all French'. But this excessively low valuation aroused the suspicions of Messrs Robson and Gibbs, Officers of the Warehouse, who impounded the chairs and referred the matter to their superiors. Within a few days the authorities had satisfied themselves of Chippendale's culpability, and had given directions for the appropriate action to be taken — not, as in our own time, confiscation and even graver consequences, but an amusing kind of poetic justice. In such cases the customs service bought the goods in question at the importer's own valuation, remitting duties and adding 10 per cent to the purchase price. In this way Chippendale and others like him made a quick and adequate profit on the goods they

Above: *Design for a brass handle. The* Director *(1762), Pl.CXCIX*

Opposite: *Pier glass with Chippendale* chinoiserie *gilded frame supplied to Nostell Priory in 1770. The dressing commode, japanned green and gold, was supplied by Chippendale in 1771 for the ante-room at Nostell Priory*

brought in – if their valuation proved to be correct. In practice, of course, the Commissioners for Customs were able to sell the compulsorily purchased items at a handsome profit that went to swell the funds of the service.

It is characteristic of the age that these abuses were not brought to light by official investigation, but because other cabinet-makers (that is, those who were not in on the deal) complained and pressed for government action. In 1773 a parliamentary committee was told about the way in which cabinet-makers were taking advantage of the diplomatic bags, and among those accused were John Cobb, Chippendale's near neighbour at 72 St Martin's Lane, and James Cullen of Greek Street; at the time, the standing and clientele of these men were on par with Chippendale's, providing another confirmation that his legal peccadillos were not particularly unusual.

Garrick

Chippendale's name was not mentioned, but he was indirectly affected by the enquiry and the attendant publicity, which seem to have made the customs officials more active. Since there was nothing they could do about the importation of illicit goods in the diplomatic bags, they tried to impede their distribution by making periodic raids on cabinet-makers' shops; and on one such occasion in the 1770s Chippendale was found in possession of a large quantity of Indian chintz, which was promptly confiscated; the importing of Indian printed cottons was strictly forbidden in order to protect English manufacturers. The material in question actually belonged to the famous actor David Garrick and his wife, who had sent it to Chippendale to make up into hangings for an 'oriental' bedroom, so Chippendale was not the most culpable party in the affair – although Mrs Garrick seems to have thought so, at least in the sense that she was inclined to blame him for being found out. Her draft of a letter to Chippendale, complaining about this and her other dealings with the firm, was written in 1778, but it is not clear whether her reproaches concerning the Indian chintz refer to the immediate past or some remoter period, since she was angry enough to list every grievance she could think of, threatening to call in a valuer for an opinion on everything Chippendale had made for her since 1772, some six years earlier. It must remain an open question whether this also means that the Garricks had not settled his bill since that date!

Before pursuing Chippendale's career, one isolated piece of information needs to be mentioned. 'Thomas Chippindale of St Martin's Lane London Cabinet Maker' is named as a party to a legal transaction – indentures of lease and release, dated 30 April and 1 May 1770 – concerning a house and orchard in Boroughgate, Otley. The surviving document is only a kind of summary, so it is not clear just what role Chippendale played, though it seems possible that he was investing money in the property, if only by way of helping out his cousin, William Chippendale of Farnley. This suggests that Chippendale's cash crisis

Above: Bed supplied in 1775 to Garrick's villa at Hampton. The bedstead is japanned in green and white. Victoria and Albert Museum

at the beginning of the 1770s may have been less severe than his letters indicate; but in the absence of any other evidence no firm interpretation of the Boroughgate affair is possible. The real significance of the document, which was first brought to light in 1912, is that it proves beyond reasonable doubt that Thomas Chippendale the Otley joiner's son was the same person as Thomas Chippendale of St Martin's Lane. It also suggests that he kept in close touch with his native town and his numerous relatives, another two of whom were involved in the lease and release.

A professional disagreement

From the 1760s onwards Chippendale worked for dozens of wealthy patrons and came into contact with the leading architects of the day, who included Sir William Chambers, James Wyatt and Robert Adam. The most important of these relationships, known through business letters and accounts, are discussed in a later chapter (see page 110 onwards), but we do get a glimpse of Chippendale himself in a series of minor disputes that developed around the furnishing of Melbourne House. This was the town house of Viscount Melbourne, built for him by Sir William Chambers; it has survived to the present day under the name Albany, functioning as a block of flats and forming a quiet enclave just off Piccadilly. Like other architects of period, Chambers was concerned to secure a decorative scheme in harmony with his designs, and on 14 August 1773 he wrote a long letter of complaint to Melbourne, his main grievance being that

Chippendale called upon me yesterday with some designs for furnishing the rooms which upon the whole seem very well; but I wish to be a little consulted about these matters as I am really a very pretty connoisseur in furniture. Be pleased, therefore, if it is agreeable to your Lordship and my Lady, to order him to show me the drawings at large for the tables, glasses &c before they are put in hand, as I think from his small drawings that some parts may be improved a little.

I do not like the method of fitting up my Lady's dressing room with girandoles and a glass out of centre and the girandoles quite irregularly placed. Pictures would be much better, and in the great room fewer sofas and more chairs would be better than as Chippendale has designed. I have now all the paintings ready for the Drawing Room Ceiling . . .

Above: *Robert Adam. National Portrait Gallery*

Sir William Chambers

Several interesting conclusions can be drawn from this letter. The most obvious is that Chambers was intent on establishing his overall responsibility for furnishing Melbourne House, and became extremely touchy as soon as he felt his authority threatened. This was not just a perfectionist's determination to make sure that every detail was right: the mock-modest language is unmistakably that of wounded vanity. It is also fairly clear that Chambers wanted to put Chippendale in his place — that of an inferior who executed orders rather than made creative decisions. (Later in the same letter Chambers wrote loftily that 'I desired Chippendale to show your Lordship some door scutcheons [keyhole plates] for the principal apartments which are handsome and come very reasonably', thus implying that Chippendale was above all a tradesman who could be sent round to display his wares.) On the other hand Chambers would not risk his authority by ordering Chippendale to show him his 'drawings at large' (detailed drawings intended for the use of the craftsmen), but tried to get Melbourne to do it for him.

The language used by Chippendale in the first edition of the *Director* shows that he had a just appreciation of his own abilities; but his letters reveal an equally clear understanding that he must behave with the subservience expected of a tradesman. There is the added point that no one else is mentioned as supplying furniture to Melbourne House, so this was an important commission.

The contrast with Chambers' manner is striking, and points up the gulf in status between architect and cabinet-maker – a gulf admittedly widened by the fact that Chambers stood at the head of his profession, having been knighted in 1770. After all, in complaining about Chippendale he was indirectly rebuking Melbourne, for the offending drawings could only have been commissioned by the Viscount himself. A more irate character than Melbourne might easily have taken amiss Chambers' smoothly ironic 'wish to be a little consulted about these matters', although he may have enjoyed Chambers' remarks at the expense of those traditional butts, the servants:

Please to desire your butler to give orders about fitting up the cellar, and please to advise him to have a little mercy: your other servants have ordered so many cupboards, shelves, drawers, presses &c. &c. that one would imagine there was to be a fair in every room.

Below: *A contemporary gilt mirror and occasional table*

Lord Melbourne

There was another passage of arms in October of the following year, when Melbourne gave his verdict on the way in which a first-floor lobby should be furnished. Writing very much as though it was Chambers who had to be kept in good humour, Melbourne said that in this room 'in which you have exceeded my utmost wish' he was 'more and more averse to admit any gilding whatever, even in the furniture' and had therefore

> *stopped the gilding of any of the things for that room at Chippendale's, although some few things were done but I had rather give that up, so that we may make the room all perfection.*

It is not clear whether Melbourne had now repented of an earlier decision to gild the furniture, taken under Chambers' influence, or whether Chambers had gone ahead and ordered the gilding from Chippendale on his own responsibility.

Gilded furniture

The sequel is remarkable, in that Chambers persisted in his opinion and tried to impose it on his client. In a letter dated 22 October 1774 he wrote of going to Melbourne's house 'with Chippendale's men, who brought the glasses and some of the chairs that I might see the effect of the gilding in the round room'; presumably these were the chairs that had been gilded before Melbourne vetoed the idea. If Chambers' expression of regret at having just missed Melbourne is sincere, he intended to prove his point to the Viscount in the most direct fashion by showing him that gilding worked. Chambers went on to insist politely ('it is, I think, clear') that glasses, sofas and chairs should all be gilded. He also criticized the chairs as too small for the decorative scheme ('armchairs would have answered much better'), which must mean that this was another point on which he had not been consulted. No further discussions on the subject are recorded, but it is known that Melbourne stood firm, deciding that white painted furniture was what he wanted in his round room.

This episode highlights the difference between the architect–client and cabinet-maker–client relationships: the well-established architect could talk back to his patron in a way that the well-established cabinet-maker would never dare to do. Although Chippendale figures in all this, the exact nature of his role is not easy to make out. On the surface the argument in 1774 was between Chambers and Melbourne, with Chippendale's workmen gilding or desisting from gilding according to their latest instructions from the client or his architect. However, the earlier contretemps between Chambers and Chippendale makes it clear that working directly for Melbourne left the cabinet-maker greater creative freedom; so Chambers' blunt remark about the chairs being too small may have been directed at Chippendale as the person actually responsible for any item that had not been previously approved by the architect.

Chippendale appears to have worked on steadily through it all, getting the job

Above: *Sir William Chambers, one of the leading architects of the day. His portrait can be seen in the National Portrait Gallery*

done in whatever form it presented itself. After all, in his time he had not only designed furniture with relatively few constraints (for clients willing to take expert advice, and also for the *Director*), but had also on occasion resigned himself to simply executing designs by other men – the architect Robert Adam, for example. (By contrast, Sir William Chambers, however critical as a 'connoisseur', never drew his own furniture designs.) From this point of view Chippendale behaved just like the tradesman he was supposed to be. Despite his gifts he was evidently a practical man: he did what he could to improve his artistic standing, but for the most part he took the world as he found it and did the work that came to his hand.

The last years

Of Chippendale's personal life we know only the barest details. By his wife Catherine Redshaw he had nine children, all of them born between 1749 and 1761, and all but the eldest entered in the baptismal register of St Martin-in-the-Fields. Catherine died in 1772, and five years later, in August 1777, the fifty-nine-year-old Chippendale married again. His second wife, Elizabeth Davies, gave him three children in just over two years of marriage, the first (arriving in December 1777) evidently conceived several months before the wedding, and the third born in June 1780, seven months after Chippendale's death. Of his twelve offspring, only four were alive by 1784, a not uncommon situation in a period when the death-rate was high and children were particularly at risk.

The parish records in which these events are recorded suggest that by 1777 Chippendale no longer lived in St Martin's Lane: he was married in the parish church at Fulham, still a village west of London rather than a suburb; his children by Elizabeth Davis were baptized at St Mary Abbot's, on the corner of Kensington Church Street, rather closer to the metropolis; and Chippendale himself died right on the other side of London, at Hoxton, north of the City, where he and his wife were living in lodgings. This suggests that he had retired at some point in the late 1770s, allowing his eldest son Thomas to take over the business and the living accommodation in St Martin's Lane.

Thomas had certainly been involved in the firm from at least as far back as 1767, and did in fact carry on as Haig's partner after his father's death. But Chippendale's retirement can only have been partial, since he was still corresponding on behalf of the firm in 1778, and legal documents make it clear that he retained a financial interest to the last.

Thomas Chippendale's body was taken back to St Martin-in-the-Fields for burial on 13 November 1779. The sexton noted that he was 'Consp M. 62 yrs Thomas Chippendale St Martin's Lane N.O.G. and prays £2.7.4.', which tells us not only the price of the interment, but that Chippendale was a consumptive male, was buried in the North Old Ground (roughly where the National Gallery now stands), and that prayers were said for him. Eight days later, Chippendale's own domestic furniture was examined by two 'sworn appraisers' who valued it at exactly £28 2s 9d.

Above right: *Original drawing of the salon sofa designed by Robert Adam for Sir Lawrence Dundas, signed and dated 1764.*

Below right: *One of the suite of four sofas which Sir Lawrence Dundas commissioned from Chippendale, to Robert Adam's design (above) for the salon at his London house, No 19 Arlington Street. It is the only time when Chippendale is definitely known to have executed one of Adam's furniture designs, although it is not a slavish copy*

A detail from the Diana and Minerva commode, Harewood House

Chapter Five

FURNITURE BY CHIPPENDALE

Because of the popularity of the Chippendale style, and the number of designs in the *Director*, identifying Chippendale's own furniture is no easy task. Chippendale and Robert Adam collaborated on several great houses like Harewood House, Dumfries House and Nostell Priory which are regarded as showcases for them both. Adam was strongly influenced by the Neo-Classical movement which gradually replaced the vogue for Rococo, and Chippendale in turn made a similar transition. Neo-Classical features, particularly the use of marquetry, were to emerge as distinctive characteristics of his work.

A fairly large number of pieces in the *Director* or 'Chippendale' style are still in existence, having survived changes of fashion, wars, accidents and wear and tear; and while some of these may be independent works in the Rococo–Chinese–Gothic vein, there are also many striking 'book pieces' which are more or less directly based on Chippendale's published designs. This is, of course, far from proving that such furniture was made by Chippendale's firm. The opposite is in fact the case: the very success of the *Director* has made it more difficult to identify Chippendale's own furniture, since anything he is known to have designed could in principle have been made by other firms or individuals with access to his book, either in London or in the provinces, or even abroad.

Chippendale or 'Chippendale'?

As a result, experts are particularly insistent, where early work by Chippendale is concerned, that all furniture attributed to him must be authenticated by contemporary documents naming him, which not only means that the furniture and documents must exist, but that there must be a proven link between the two. Other kinds of circumstantial evidence are sometimes admitted, but only when they are very convincing indeed.

The evidence

Most of the documents with any claim to relevance are of three kinds. There are the household accounts or personal records kept by the occupants or staff of houses which Chippendale supplied with furniture; the itemized bills sent to clients by Chippendale's firm; and, in a handful of instances, the letters exchanged between the clients and Chippendale (or, on occasion, his partner Thomas Haig, or Thomas Chippendale the younger). These have provided a good deal of fascinating information about Chippendale's activities, his whereabouts at certain periods, the running of his business and his relationship with the people he worked for; and his bills are prime evidence for the scale on which the upper classes were prepared to purchase furnishings in order to live in appropriately modish splendour. However, the existence of documentation does not remove all problems of authentication, since documents represent only one side of the equation: they can only begin to be related to surviving pieces of furniture if the furniture stands in, or can be traced back to, the same establishment as the documents. And this, although not unknown, occurs infrequently in the early '*Director*' phase of Chippendale's career, although, fortunately, one magnificent collection does survive and is almost fully accounted for.

Before passing on to this, it is worth exploring the question of attributions a little further. At first sight, the expert's criteria may seem needlessly exacting; but this is true only in the sense that the

Opposite: *This nineteenth century Chinese cabinet is an exact copy of a design in the* Director *(1754), Pl.CVI. Shugborough Hall, Staffordshire*

Right: *A Chippendale ribband-backed chair*

fine furniture of a period is what really matters, and its quality is unaffected by whether it turns out to have been made by Chippendale or by competing firms such as Vile and Cobb. However, the desire to establish authorship has proved irrepressible in this as in all studies in the arts, and in the long run it does lead to greater appreciation of those qualities that differentiate one particular artist or craftsman from others working in a seemingly identical style.

'Book pieces'

Where Chippendale is concerned, the quest, if undertaken at all, must be pursued with great caution, as experts have learned the hard way. Not so long ago it seemed reasonable to attribute furniture to Chippendale, even in the absence of documents, where there was a strong tradition that he had worked at a historic family house, or where a contemporary magnate or gentleman with 'Chippendale' furniture showed a strong interest in his designs. But this proved to be a mistake. The Duke of Beaufort, for example, was one of the subscribers to the first edition of the *Director*, and his home at Badminton House contained many 'book pieces' which it seemed natural to suppose were made by Chippendale. Yet the most famous pieces, a superb bed and other bedroom furniture in the Chinese style (now in the Victoria and Albert Museum, London), turned out to be by another cabinet-maker, William Linnell; once this was known, the book pieces at Badminton started to look less like the plates of the *Director*! Since the

discovery little more than twenty years ago of Linnell's authorship, even the neatest circumstantial evidence has inevitably been viewed with a certain suspicion.

Household accounts also reveal the defects of some perfectly natural assumptions about the authorship of Chippendale furniture. At Dumfries House, which Chippendale quite certainly supplied with quantities of furniture, the Earl nonetheless also employed an Edinburgh cabinet-maker to execute a sideboard after one of the designs in the *Director* — a piece that, but for the record, it would therefore be natural to associate with all the other Chippendale in the house. So even the fact that Thomas Chippendale worked for a client does not prove that all the *Director* furniture in the house is by him. The Earl was probably trying to save money on charges and transport by employing an Edinburgh man rather than a fashionable London firm. And the Duke of Atholl seems to have taken the idea a little further, since there is evidence to suggest that, having bought a fine pair of gilded candlestands for Blair Castle from Chippendale (as itemized in the cabinet-maker's bill), the Duke shrewdly employed a local craftsman to provide at least one more pair, which he

Opposite: Chinese bed from Badminton House, Gloucestershire, now in the Victoria and Albert Museum. Originally attributed to Chippendale, it is now considered to be the work of William Linnell, another cabinet-maker

could carve and gild with Chippendale's originals right in front of him.

In such extreme cases differences of quality are generally visible, but they do demonstrate that the experts' rigorous approach to authentication is far from misplaced. This does not of course mean that tentative attributions are not still made, but the line between fact and speculation is drawn very finely indeed. To some extent the problems outlined above apply to every phase of Chippendale's career. But they are most keenly felt in the phase down to about the mid-1760s, when we might have hoped to find an abundance of Rococo, Chinese and Gothic pieces by Chippendale, carrying out or comprising variations on the style of the *Director*. Instead, the record is disappointingly thin. Apart from the single allusion to Chippendale in Burlington's account-book, his earliest known commissions date from April 1757 – exactly three years after the publication of the *Director*. This is extremely puzzling, even on the theory that Chippendale was quite unknown until the book made his reputation; for if that were so, why should there be no recorded commissions for a further three years? What makes it all the stranger is that from 1757 the record is relatively full and continuous (some twenty known clients by 1764), even if not much furniture can be identified from the bills and other documents that have come to light.

Dumfries House

The earliest known Chippendale pieces are the candlestands for the Duke of Atholl and 'a firescreen of fine French tapestry with a neat mahogany pillar and claw', also for Blair Castle; for these Chippendale charged a total of £11 2s 6d in a bill dated 8 May 1758. Less than a year later came the outstanding commission of his abbreviated '*Director* period', when the firm began to supply very large quantities of goods to furnish Dumfries House. Many of these are particularly close to *Director* designs and, it is surmised, for an interesting reason. The Earl of Dumfries needed to furnish the grand new house in Ayrshire designed for him by the Adam brothers, but this was not easy to do at such a distance from London. Eventually he made up his mind to pay a brief visit to the capital and meet his requirements by ordering ready-made furniture from Chippendale and Rannie; this is inferred from the fact that, a couple of months later, the firm was shipping furniture to Scotland in quantities that could not possibly have been specially made in such a short time. And so, whereas most of Chippendale's designs for his wealthier clients were custom-made, the furniture at Dumfries House represents standard quality stock for which it would have been only natural to use the *Director* as a pattern-book.

The first and largest single consignment was dispatched in May 1759 and cost the Earl £573 16s 8d, boxed in 2,000 feet of 'glued packing case', and the charge for these and other packing materials was over £35. Chippendale also executed commissions for Dumfries House in 1763 and 1766.

Almost all the furniture he sent has

Neo-Classicism became popular in the second half of the eighteenth century. The elaborate carvings and ornamental curves of the Rococo gave way to much more restricted carvings and refined shapes.

Above: *The state dressing room at Nostell Priory is an example*

Above: *This magnificent mahogany violin bookcase was supplied to the Earl of Pembroke*

'French commode' which may have been imported by Chippendale and an unusual rosewood bookcase, described in Chippendale's invoice as having 'rich carved and gilt ornaments on the top and doors, a writing drawer in the under-part, and a clothes-press and drawers at each end'; at £45 5s it was the most expensive single piece of furniture supplied. There was also one piece specifically linked to the *Director* – the bedstead which, in a note to Plate XXXIX of the third edition, Chippendale asserted 'had been made for the Earls of Dumfries and Morton'. The Dumfries bed is a splendid object, hung with green silk and worsted damask, and 'with a dome top ornamented in the inside, the feetposts fluted and a palmbranch twisting round, and carved capitals, a carved headboard, a strong burnished rod and strong triple wheel castors'.

Chinoiserie is represented at Dumfries House by a delightful clothes-press japanned with Chinese landscapes in gold on a black ground; but the only significant Gothic element is the tracery design on the front legs of a breakfast table. Among the many other items, the carvers' pieces must be mentioned, since most of them closely resemble plates in the *Director*, and their superb carving constituted a final proof that Chippendale's designs were not 'so many specious drawings, impossible to be worked off by any Mechanick whatsoever'; they included an overmantel mirror, two large girandoles, two large oval pier glasses and a large 'lanthorn' now in the Philadelphia Museum of Art.

survived, and almost all of it is still at Dumfries House. Among the long list of items were fourteen elbow chairs and a pair of settees in serpentine Rococo style, a library table, a shaving table, a

Wilton House

Another important source of *Director* furniture is Wilton House in Wiltshire, the main country residence of Lord Pembroke. Apart from Dumfries and Morton, he was the only other patron mentioned in the third edition of the *Director*, in which a note to Plate XLVI reads, 'This couch was made for an alcove in Lord Pembroke's house at Whitehall' (known as Pembroke House). Unfortunately, although between 1763 and 1773 Chippendale received the considerable sum of £1,500 from Pembroke, this is only documented by a bare list of payments. As a result, the quantities of Rococo furniture at Wilton and Pembroke House (all now at Wilton) are mostly impossible to attribute with certainty to Chippendale, although the probability that he made many of the *Director*-style pieces is very strong. Of the half a dozen exceptions that can be attributed to him with certainty, easily the best known is the 'violin' bookcase, which draws on elements from two plates in the *Director*. This is one of the most splendid of all Chippendale's creations a large, extraordinarily elegant breakfront bookcase, imposing without heaviness, which is constructed round a central desk drawer and magnificently decorated with a carved central Rococo oval dominating the front and, above it, a pleasing musical trophy and a swan-neck pediment. Other especially noteworthy items by Chippendale include two bookcases forming a suite with the 'violin' bookcase, and a fine library table.

Above: *Imposing serpentine-fronted mahogany clothes-press supplied in 1767 to Sir Rowland Winn of Nostell Priory*

Two other patrons for whom Chippendale did some of his finest work were Sir Lawrence Dundas and Sir Rowland Winn. Only some of this can be described as Rococo, since Chippendale was beginning to respond to the new Neo-Classical style in which he was to produce most of his surviving work. Dundas was a very wealthy man who spent on a lavish scale, buying and

Above: The state bedroom, Nostell Priory. Although Neo-Classicism was coming into vogue an element of chinoiserie *survived into the 1770s*

Opposite: Detail of hand-painted wallpaper in the state bedroom at Nostell Priory, the only house to preserve an original paper supplied by Chippendale

improving widely scattered properties including Moor Park in Hertfordshire and 19 Arlington Street, London; among the *Director*-style pieces he bought from Chippendale were two fine bookcases and a mahogany chest of drawers. Sir Rowland Winn inherited his baronetcy and Nostell Priory in Yorkshire from his father in 1765; he was to become a regular if not easily satisfied customer of Chippendale's, buying furniture for Nostell and also for his town house, 11 St James's Square. Generally speaking he eschewed luxury items, but among the Rococo furniture he ordered from Chippendale was one extremely expensive (£37) serpentine-fronted piece which the cabinet-maker described in his bill as 'a very large mahogany clothes-press of exceeding fine wood in a commode shape with 7 shelves in the upper part, lined with paper and green baize aprons, and 4 drawers in the underpart with best wrought handles to ditto'.

This, although sumptuous, was relatively restrained. More exuberantly Rococo pieces would soon go right out of fashion as a more sober artistic mood became dominant — a phenomenon described in the pages that follow. But although Rococo became outmoded, a degree of fantasy continued to be acceptable, since *chinoiserie* lived on into the 1770s; however, it was increasingly viewed as a kind of legitimate private frolic, most suited to the bedroom, and when used as surface decoration was applied to furniture whose form was Neo-Classical instead of Rococo. Chippendale's surviving output from the later 1760s and 1770s includes some of his most charming work: the gay, delightful bedroom suites made for Sir Rowland Winn at Nostell Priory (where even the wallpaper is still in place), Edwin Lascelles at Harewood House, and the famous actor David Garrick at his Thameside villa.

By contrast, Chippendale Gothic is so quantitatively unimpressive that it can hardly be said to decline because it seems never to have flourished. Very little of such furniture is known apart from the library bookcases with Gothic glazing bars on the front, executed for Nostell Priory, and 'a very neat new frame' made in the Gothic style for an inlaid Indian desk belonging to Sir Edward Knatchbull of Mersham le Hatch in Kent. This is strange in view of the prominence accorded to the style in the *Director*, which gives the impression of being a publication carefully attuned to the public taste; but it is also hard to believe that sheer chance has been responsible for destroying quantities of unrecorded Gothic furniture, thus creating a false impression of Chippendale's work in the style.

Neo-Classicism

Down until very recent times, the culture of classical antiquity – ancient Greece and Rome – exercised a potent and persistent influence on the life, art and thought of the West. Classical influence was particularly striking in the visual arts, since styles inspired by antiquity – Romanesque, Renaissance, Baroque, Neo-Classicism – appeared regularly over a period of eight centuries or more. Yet no two were quite the same, for new information and different emphases changed the interpretation put on the classical tradition; and, even more important, classicism was made to serve a different set of moods and needs, so that each classicizing movement was unlike the others in its atmosphere and tone. Thus in the 18th century, Baroque gave way for a few decades to the anti-classical, asymmetrical Rococo style; but when Rococo in turn was replaced by a resurgence of classicism, there was no return to the imposing, dramatic, spatially dynamic quality of Baroque: the victorious Neo-Classical movement had a lighter, more contained and more suavely elegant air than its older relation.

The renewed interest in all things classical became very apparent in western Europe from about 1750, when it was reinforced by the sensational results of excavations at the buried cities of Pompeii and Herculaneum, and by the publication of influential books of engravings showing the antiquities of Rome, Baalbek and Palmyra.

Robert Adam

One of the many artists who felt impelled to examine some of these on the spot was the Scottish architect Robert Adam, who spent four years studying in Italy and among the imperial Roman remains on the Dalmatian coast. On his return in 1758 Adam quickly established himself as one of the most influential figures of his time. His subsequent publications, and above all his practice as an artist and designer, gave British Neo-Classicism its distinctive character, at once light, rich and restrained.

Whereas most architects were content to design buildings, leaving their furnishings to others, Adam realized the importance, especially in domestic architecture, of creating interiors that were unified in style, in harmony with the dwelling, and yet interestingly diversified. As the greatest interior decorator of his time, Adam succeeded in creating a style of civilized opulence, based on painted, gilded or stuccoed low relief, that can still be seen in such famous houses as Harewood House, Osterley Park and Kenwood.

The impact on cabinet-making was profound, since Neo-Classicism involved a revolution in taste and also in technique. Rococo and its allied styles had achieved their most glamorous

Above: *The amber room at Nostell Priory is a fine example of Chippendale's Neo-Classical style. The renewed interest in all things classical became apparent in Europe after 1750. In England Robert Adam was one of its chief proponents giving Neo-Classicism here its distinctive characteristics of richness and restraint*

Above: Pier table, one of a pair, made for the Music Room at Harewood House. The top is decorated with marquetry on a rosewood ground

effects by means of riotous, elaborate carving and emphatic curves. We have seen that Chippendale greatly widened the decorative vocabulary of the *Director* in its third edition of 1762 by introducing classical motifs; but the shape of his furniture was largely unaffected. However, in Adam's hands Neo-Classicism became an all-embracing style in which the serpentine and *bombé* had no part. Carving was restricted and the outlines of furniture were simplified and refined; tapered and fluted supports replaced the cabriole leg, and chairs were made with oval-, shield-, heart- or lyre-shaped backs (the lyre, of course, being an 'antique' instrument).

Veneers and marquetry

The surfaces of pieces were lavishly enriched with veneers and marquetry. Veneering was done by glueing thinly-cut slices of wood on to the surfaces of the basic piece of furniture. This meant that rare or expensive woods could be used in small quantities, enabling the cabinet-maker to create an impression of opulence at a relatively low cost; but it also made more sophisticated effects possible, since strips from the same tree, with identical markings, could be arranged in sets of two or four to form symmetrical patterns. Marquetry was even more elaborate, consisting of patterns or pictures made from woods of various shapes and colours, which were inlaid into the veneer. It was done by placing two or more pieces of veneer on top of one another and cutting through them in the required pattern, using a fine saw; the 'jigsaw pieces' produced in this fashion could then be arranged into one or more versions of the pattern.

Despite its neglect during the Rococo period, marquetry was revived with extraordinary success, and its use on furniture by Chippendale and some of his contemporaries remains unsurpassed. The woods used for making furniture also change to suit the new mood; the dominance of mahogany was challenged by tulipwood and rosewood, and at the height of Adam's vogue all three gave way to satinwood, whose rippling creamy surface toned in wonderfully with the pale splendours of Adam interiors.

Although used relatively sparingly, carving, gilding and painting still

Below: *The crimson bedchamber by Robert Adam at Nostell Priory.*

formed part of the decoration of furniture, which was also frequently enriched – and protected – by gilt ormolu mounts after the French fashion. The 'vocabulary' of the decoration was supplied from classical sources, somewhat modified by Renaissance influences; in addition to various motifs mentioned earlier, these included anthemion or honeysuckle blossoms, round or oval discs (paterae) or medallions, chains of husks and loops of knotted ribbons. Taken all together, the restrained, refined forms, the surfaces with veneering and marquetry, the use of gilt mounts and the husk-, ribbon- and honeysuckle-draped classical motifs give Neo-classical furniture its quite distinctive appearance – one that might have been produced in a different century or culture from the Rococo and other exotic styles.

Robert Adam's influence

Chippendale, like other artists and designers, made the transition from Rococo to Neo-Classicism over a period of years, and some of his finest work combines elements from both styles. Adam almost certainly influenced him, for many of Chippendale's commissions entailed the supply of furniture to houses built or remodelled by the Scottish architect; and Adam's concern with unity of effect makes it certain that he would (where still employed by the client) have scrutinized Chippendale's designs. At one time scholars were inclined to believe that Adam himself was responsible for all the furniture in his houses, and that Chippendale and other cabinet-makers were merely employed to execute his designs. But while it is true that Adam did design some furniture – brilliantly if not always professionally – it is now generally held that he concerned himself mainly with the more or less fixed wall furniture (consoles, mirrors, etc.) which gave a room its atmosphere. No doubt he supervised or was consulted about other arrangements, and there is nothing particularly demeaning to Chippendale in supposing that Adam made a helpful creative contribution to his work. However, the fact that Chippendale produced superb furniture for houses unconnected with Adam suggests that his debt to the latter was primarily stylistic.

Like the practical man he was, Chippendale evidently reconciled himself to working to another man's designs rather than lose custom; for in a single known case he quite certainly made furniture from a design by Robert Adam. Both the date and the client are significant. The design – for a sofa – was drawn in 1764 for Sir Lawrence Dundas: it therefore represents the very latest fashion, interpreted by its chief promoter and paid for by an exceptionally rich, socially ambitious man who wanted his London house to be the last word in modernity. (In the best 18th-century fashion Dundas had made his great wealth from army contracts.) This suggests that it may have been an exceptional event, for few clients can have been willing to pay Adam's very high fee (£5 for a single drawing) once Chippendale, who charged nothing for his designs, had

familiarized himself with the new style!

This and other furniture made for Dundas in 1765 is particularly interesting, since it is possible to see the difference in styles between two suites that were made almost simultaneously by Chippendale. For the Long Room at Arlington Street, Dundas ordered ten French armchairs and three matching sofas in third-edition *Director* style, essentially Rococo with some classical details. But for the grandest place in the house, the Great Room, he paid Adam for the design mentioned above, which became the basis for a suite made by

Above: Giltwood armchair upholstered in red figured silk. One of a set of eight designed by Robert Adam and executed by Chippendale. Victoria and Albert Museum

Chippendale – four sofas and eight armchairs replete with classical motifs, though still not entirely deprived of Rococo curves. Both suites are sumptuous, but the difference between them in this respect is reflected in the prices (£235 and £376). Stylistic transitions are more apparent to posterity than to contemporaries, and it should cause no

Above: *Detail from the large mahogany library table (1766), decorated with carved lions' heads and paws, made for Nostell Priory. It is regarded as one of Chippendale's finest pieces*

surprise to learn that the more 'advanced' design seems to have been ordered before the Rococo suite; at any rate Chippendale invoiced for them respectively in July 1765 and January 1766. However, his own stylistic awareness is indicated by the July bill, in which the chairs are described as 'exceeding Richly carv'd in the Antick manner' – the first recorded occasion on which he uses 'Antick' or 'Antique', terms that he would henceforth employ frequently.

Some of Chippendale's finest furniture dates from the later 1760s, when he was moving towards Neo-Classicism without having completely shed his earlier style. Easily the most celebrated piece from this period is the superbly carved library table made in 1767 for Sir Rowland Winn of Nostell Priory. As so often, Chippendale himself gives the best description in his invoice, combining a breathless factuality with a touch delighted self-praise:

a large mahogany library table of very fine wood with doors on each side of the bottom part and drawers within on one side and partitions on the other, with terms of ditto carved and ornamented with lions' heads and paws, with carved ovals in the panels of the doors and the top covered with black leather, and the whole completely finished in the most elegant taste.

The number of surviving pieces of Chippendale furniture in a more or less Neo-Classical style is substantially greater than that known from his *Direc-*

tor period. Paradoxically, this fact has led to a further enlargement of the Chippendale canon, since a bigger 'sample' has made it possible for experts to identify certain common characteristics, visible in details of design and workmanship; and these can serve as a basis for attributing additional, less firmly documented pieces to Chippendale. From this point of view the absence of a Neo-Classical edition of the *Director* is a positive advantage, making it less likely that Chippendale lookalikes of this later period might be copies by other cabinet-makers.

An exhaustive list of Chippendale furniture in the Neo-Classical style is neither possible nor desirable here. But although our attention inevitably fixes on a few masterpieces, it is well to remember that Chippendale produced furniture of all kinds, and also of varying degrees of luxuriousness. Despite the existence at Nostell Priory of pieces

Above: *Counter thought to have been made for the apothecary's shop at Nostell Priory. Chippendale was always prepared to make good quality, plain furniture*

such as the famous library table and, oddly enough, a magnificent Neo-Classical barometer, most of the furniture supplied by Chippendale was of good quality but far from luxurious; and here and elsewhere he was always ready to make quantities of good plain utility furniture for non-genteel use.

Apart from Nostell, Chippendale had major commissions in the late 1760s and the 1770s at a number of houses which still contain at least some furniture by him. These include Harewood House, Newby and Burton Constable, all (like Nostell) in Yorkshire; Paxton in Berwickshire; and Petworth in Sussex. At some other houses (notably Mersham le Hatch in Kent and Melbourne House in London) the furniture has gone but surviving documents have made it possible to track down some pieces. And of course there are a good many other places where a few items survive or have been traced to new domiciles; and

Below: *The Diana and Minerva dressing commode at Harewood House*

Right: *Clock, the* Director, *Pl. CLXVI*

others still where documents hint at, record or even describe furniture that it has not so far been possible to trace.

Harewood House

In monetary terms the greatest commission of Chippendale's career was for Harewood House. It has been estimated that his firm eventually received in excess of £10,000 for the work done, although the owner, Edwin Lascelles, paid with such excruciating slowness (at one point running up a debt of over £6,000) that the commission must also have been one of Chippendale's greatest headaches. Artistically, however, it was a wonderful opportunity, for Lascelles seems to have given Chippendale his head and to have placed his trust completely in the one firm; unlike so many houses where Chippendale worked, Harewood has no reference to any rival metropolitan cabinet-maker in its extensive archives. Here Chippendale created a marvellous collection of luxury 'Antick' furniture, most of which was put away when it went out of fashion and has therefore survived. Some pieces have been disposed of, notably a celebrated rosewood library table sold for a record £43,050 in 1965, but an astonishing amount is still at Harewood, constituting an incomparable hoard of Chippendale treasures.

Of these the *chef d'oeuvre* is the 'Diana and Minerva commode', so called because of the figures of the two goddesses in marquetry medallions of coloured woods and ivory on the doors. This immensely luxurious piece, veneered with satinwood and profusely inlaid, is

justly famous, although Chippendale did some similarly opulent pieces for other clients; these, the 'Renishaw commode' and the 'Panshanger cabinets', are undocumented, and it is their affinity with the 'Diana and Minerva commode' that has led to their inclusion in the Chippendale canon. It seems appropriate to end this chapter with Chippendale's own characteristic description of his most famous piece, invoiced on 12 November 1773; his lengthy remarks may indicate pride in achievement – or the need to justify the high price:

A very large rich Commode with exceeding fine Antique Ornaments curiously inlaid with various fine woods – Drawers at each End and enclosed with folding Doors, with Diana and Minerva and their Emblems Curiously inlaid & Engraved, a Cupboard in the middle part with a Cove [concave] Door, a Dressing Drawer in the Top part, the whole Elegantly Executed & Varnished, with many wrought Brass Antique Ornaments finely finished £86

Detail of a Chippendale writing table, Stourhead, Wiltshire, showing carved heads of philosophers

Chapter Six

THE FIRM AND ITS CUSTOMERS

Chippendale was justly proud of the comprehensive service he offered his customers, which included moving, storing, repairing and cleaning furniture and upholstery, as well as supplying it. No detail was too small, and Chippendale was in the habit of corresponding personally with his clients, who put great trust in his taste and ability. Many of these letters make fascinating reading and have been put to good use by scholars researching into this master craftsman about whose life relatively little is known, whose authenticated works are relatively few, but whose reputation is even greater now than in his own lifetime.

Thomas Chippendale was neither a bench-bound craftsman nor an artist in the sense of being an independent creator: he was the head of a large, complicated business operation. His surviving designs, neat and often charmingly coloured, look like the results of a tranquil creativity; but in fact we must picture him frequently on the move, coping with a variety of practical problems, and responding creatively to fortuitous situations ('As to the border for the India paper, I cannot get a neat one so I have drawd a new design and it is making'). A number of references in his letters prove that Chippendale travelled widely in England, as far north as his native Yorkshire, though not, apparently, to Scotland, despite the number of the firm's Scottish clients, probably acquired through Rannie's business and family links with Edinburgh. (However, given the state of the roads, this is not altogether surprising.) When any big commission came up, Chippendale went to the house to consult with the owner and/or architect, advise and measure up; we get a glimpse of a particularly propitious beginning in a letter he wrote to Sir Rowland Winn in July 1767, describing his first visit to Harewood House:

as soon as I had got to Mr Lascelles and looked over the whole of the house I found that [I] should want . . . many designs, and knowing that I had time enough I went to York to do them.

The premises and stock

But, even with the help of partners who were more financially astute, running the firm must have taken up a good deal of Chippendale's time. The St Martin's Lane premises were by no means the biggest cabinet-makers in London, but their extent is nonetheless surprising, as we know from a plan made in 1803 for the Sun Insurance Company; although this was over twenty years after Chippendale's death, the firm was being run by his son and there is no reason to suppose that there had been any major changes.

The three dwellings on St Martin's Lane hid a complex of brick and timber structures stretching a long way back and surrounding two separate yards; access was by means of a wagon-way between the houses. Apart from these, the plan indicates the existence of counting rooms, store rooms, a chair room, a drying room for deal planks, a carpet room, a veneering room, two feather rooms (for upholstery), a [mirror] glass room, a three-storey cabinet-maker's shop right at the back, an upholsterer's shop, various 'ware-rooms' and a very large area beneath the

Opposite: *A detail of the canopy of a George III fourposter Chippendale bed at Harewood House. The bed is painted blue, with parcel gilt*

Right: *Posts and part of the lower canopy from the same George III fourposter bed, recently sold by Christie's at Harewood House, Yorkshire*

Above: *Detail of the sliding shelves lined with marbled paper from the serpentine-fronted clothes-press at Nostell Priory*

roof of a long building where wood was stored. Other types of work may have been performed, but some were certainly put out to independent specialists. A letter from Chippendale to Winn

indicates that in his day this was the case with gilding, dyeing and making wallpaper; whether some or all of the carving or marquetry for his furniture was done on the premises is not known.

These ample premises were needed to house the workforce and to maintain an adequate supply of timber and ready-made items in order to execute commissions and meet the demands of on-the-spot buyers. The formidable quantity of stock involved is known from the auction list of 1766. Along with wages and other expenses, it represents a heavy investment and high running costs, so it is not surprising that Chippendale suffered intermittently from cash-flow problems when clients such as Edwin Lascelles ran up huge bills and could not be induced to pay.

An all-in service

No doubt Chippendale's profit margin was high in order to compensate for these drawbacks; and the firm was geared to do any and every sort of work remotely connected with furniture and furnishing, from supplying master-pieces of carving and marquetry to 'Repairing the Vinitian Sun blinds' at Harewood or packing up and sending a mangle. In effect, Chippendale provided an all-embracing furnishing service, supplying luxury and utility furniture, covers, curtains, drapes, pelmets, mattresses, blankets, counter-panes, shelves, wallpaper, sham books for library doors (81 at 6d: £2 0s 6d), soap cups, bells barometers, tassels . . . Chippendale & Co. would store a client's furniture (4s 6d a week for Sir

William Robertson) while they prepared his new house for him; would supervise moving operations (thirty cartloads of David Garrick's furniture and the stationing of a night watchman at his new home); and would clean, repair or alter upholstery and furniture to order. On one occasion the firm was charged with organizing a funeral, and the itemized invoice for £121 15s 11d gives a fascinating insight into a great aristocratic ceremonial occasion, with Chippendale & Haig supplying fine ostrich feathers and velvet coverings for the hearse and horses, a luxuriously lined coffin, and quantities of silk hatbands and kid gloves for tenants, servants and under-bearers.

Sending goods and materials required careful packing, and the state of the roads was such that it was cheaper and safer to use a boat if the client lived anywhere near navigable waters; even

Sir Edward Knatchbull in Kent obtained furniture in this way. A letter to the Earl of Dumfries by Chippendale and Rannie tells us that the goods sent by 'the diligence which sailed on Sunday morning early' were insured for £700 ('which we hope is enough as we don't think the danger is great'). His lordship is advised that the carriage he sends to collect the goods should have 'such coverings as will turn rain lest they should meet it upon the road', despite the fact that the damask furniture was packed in glued cases. And one of Chippendale's men went with: 'The contents of each case with proper directions are given to the person who goes to put up the furniture. We pay him a guinea a week and we make no

Below: Folded library steps concealed as a long stool. Nostell Priory

doubt but he will acquit himself with your Lordship's approbation.'

Attention to details

At houses that were not quite so distant, a number of Chippendale's men might be installed, and at Harewood they were employed intermittently for years, performing a thousand and one tasks as recorded by Lascelles' conscientious steward in his day book. A small selection comprises papering the Bamboo Cotton room and 'unpacking and fixing furniture' for it, 'sheeting up the beds and taking down the window curtains

Below: Thomas Chippendale is known as a designer of furniture but he also designed these borders for fabric or wallpaper. The Director *(1762), Pl.CXCV*

&c.', stuffing the chairs for the coffee and billiard room, 'going to Leeds to buy paper for the women servants' rooms', lining the inside of the plate closet, altering the pullies of the dining room window curtains, hanging the State Bed chamber with green damask, and 'taking the feathers out of beds and drying and beating them'. William Reid, an upholsterer sent to Harewood by Chippendale spent no less than twenty-four weeks and three days at the house, services for which the firm invoiced Lascelles at £29 8s – a very modest element in a bill that was already running at well over five thousand pounds.

Craftsman and customer

Chippendale was entirely responsible for this side of things, and for all

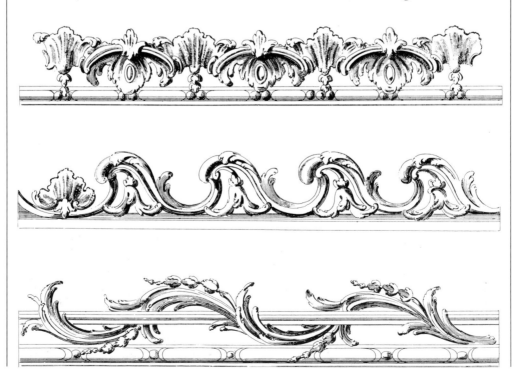

Above: *Another detail from the Chippendale writing table at Stourhead, Wiltshire*

relations with clients, as two important sets of letters confirm; his partners write only in Chippendale's absence, and even then restrict themselves to financial matters. There are twenty-six letters between Chippendale himself and Sir Rowland Winn of Nostell Priory, and seven between Chippendale and Sir Edward Knatchbull of Mersham le Hatch. They paint a none-too-happy picture of the relationship between cabinet-maker and client, although the sample they provide is far too small for us to be certain that it is typical. The existing correspondence may have been preserved just because it dealt with matters in dispute, and if similar correspondence had survived from clients such as Sir William Robinson and Edwin Lascelles, who seem to have placed great trust in Chippendale's taste and ability, the situation might look quite different.

Provided this is borne in mind, the correspondence is fascinating and infor-

Above: The drawing room, Nostell Priory. The relationship between Chippendale and Sir Rowland Winn was not always harmonious. Chippendale was kept waiting for lengthy periods of time, even years, before his bills were settled, and Winn accused Chippendale of failing repeatedly to deliver on time

mative. The common elements in the two sets are striking: the client writes with an arrogant assurance of superiority to which Chippendale replies humbly; the cabinet-maker's bills remain unsettled for years, and his complaints are received without much sympathy; and on occasion the client nevertheless complains about the size of his bill, with obscure consequences.

Correspondence with Winn

The Chippendale-Winn letters include a further element: Winn's repeated complaints about Chippendale's failure to deliver on time, and Chippendale's subsequent apologies and explanations. Over a period of three years Chippendale claims to have been ill on several occasions, to have been let down by his foreman (who supposedly disappeared into Yorkshire for six weeks), to have been distracted by sudden orders from the royal family, and to have been compelled to do other work by his need for ready cash. There are so many excuses in these letters that they fail to carry conviction as a whole, although it is perfectly possible that some are true. There is no way of knowing whether Chippendale was rather unreliable, whether Winn was unreasonable in his expectations, or whether Chippendale was simply unable to cope with the orders coming in – especially the large orders from Harewood House, which must have made Sir Rowland Winn's seem very small beer. Not that Chippendale wanted to lose the baronet's custom, as his answer to Winn's loudest explosion indicates. This exchange also demonstrates the superior–inferior relationship between them, particularly (to modern eyes) in view of the fact that the twenty-seven-year-old Winn was addressing a man who was over twenty years his senior.

He wrote:

*As your Behaviour Convinces me that you do not think My Custom & protection worth paying any Regard to, I shall endeavour to find out some other person that will be More grateful & that will not use Me in the Manner You have done which I shall not **Easily forgett** & **must** now tell You that You May Expect to find me as great an **Enemy** as I ever was Your Friend. It is not to be **Conceived** the great **Expense** & **Inconvenience** you have put me to by Your Neglect therefore as I will not be **trifled** with any longer desire you will send me My Bill immediately also the Damask Beds & Glasses with the Borders finish'd or not, As to the other Furniture that you was to have made me if they are not finish'd on the Rect of this letter you need not send them as I shall get them elsewhere the Time being long Expired that you promised to send them & that you declared if they did not come to the time you wou'd not have one Farthing for them, your Behaviour to me is not to be Bore & [I] shall take care to Acquaint those Gentlemen that I have Recommended you to & desire that they will oblige me in employing some other person.*

And Chippendale answered:

Yours of the 27th of Septr I received and I am extreamly sorry I am likely to loose you my Patron For I had taken it into my Head to think you so, but I still hope for the best and that all may be well yet, For I still will do all I can to preserve your good Graces if possible. As to any expence extraordinary that you have been at in regard to Mr Brewer I solemnly declare I had rather pay it than have any anger about it; There has been some delay in the things not being sent in time But Sr you know as well as I what difficulty there is in having things done according to time, when other workmen are Concern'd, (For God's sake consider a little good Sr Rowland An Instance or two I will take the liberty to mention to you, The first is the Damask beds which I have but got home today and it was sent to the Dyers the next day after I received them, and I dare venter to say that I & my foremen have been after them forty times but he is the best dyer in London and I wanted it well done. The next was the Gilt border it was Carvd ı Whole month before I co'ld get it Gilt tho' it might all have been Gilt in week; I do take all the blame on myself but the true reason is there is so much work in town of Various kinds that it is almost impossible to get any thing done, at any rate I have put all the people about the beds that can be & that shall be sent away directly, the bed posts are all done, the Chairs are also finishd, the moreen Window Curtains are done the Cotton also the Oval Glass frames are very forward

. . . and so on. Since Chippendale goes on to discuss future items of business, it may well be that the episode was more of a ritualized mini-drama than a serious crisis, with Winn ruffling his feathers and Chippendale making the appropriate kow-tow while remaining quite confident that there would be no further consequences.

Below: *Design for a couch bed. The Director (1762), Pl. XLVI*

Meanwhile the bill mounted over the years. Winn waxed indignant when pressed too hard, and Knatchbull told Chippendale flatly that 'as I receive my rents once a year, so I pay my trades-man's bills once a year, which is not reckoned very bad pay as the world goes; so that when the time comes round, that shall be paid also.' In reality Knatchbull settled rather less fre-quently, although he was no worse than Winn or Lascelles or the politician George Selwyn, who let over two years go by before paying the eighteen shil-lings he owed. There was evidently nothing Chippendale could do about the delays, since it would probably have been too expensive, as well as bad publicity, to seek redress through the courts. So we find Thomas Haig writing to Knatchbull that 'you would do a singular favour to Mr Chippendale by the payment of your note at present . . . but if you should be otherwise deter-

Below: A George III single couch bed attributed to Chippendale. Also shown is a pair of short posts of column form. Harewood House

Above: *Harewood House. A number of Chippendale's men were installed there and employed intermittently for a number of years performing a variety of tasks from unpacking and assembling furniture to buying wallpaper for the servants' rooms*

mined, he must submit.' At Harewood the bill reached such proportions that Chippendale actually suspended work, but the only threat of legal action was issued against David Garrick – perhaps because he was only a self-made man, or more likely because the ensuing publicity would have harmed the famous actor more than Chippendale.

Clients frequently complained that they had been overcharged, and the firm did sometimes accept less (for example from the Earl of Dumfries), presumably when it seemed advisable to take something rather than wrangle at a distance; it would be surprising if profit margins had not been adjusted beforehand to allow for such contingencies!

Chippendale may have overcharged, but it is also possible that his clients refused to take into account the effects of inflation, which were quite pronounced in the late 18th century. The outcome of such disputes is not always clear, and it is possible that an arbitrator was brought in; for Chippendale himself served in this capacity at least twice, on each occasion judging that somebody else's client had been overcharged!

Not much changed on the business side after Chippendale's death, for in July 1781 Thomas Haig found that Sir Rowland Winn, who had promised to pay the firm as soon as he reached Yorkshire, had gone abroad . . . However, it should be said that Winn, Knatchbull and the rest did eventually pay their bills; and Winn's continued patronage of the firm suggests that he was less dissatisfied than he made out. But he would undoubtedly have used very strong language indeed if anyone had hinted that posterity would remember not him but one of his evasive, needing-to-be-kept-up-to-the-mark tradespeople.

The historical record

Apart from business records and advertisements, there are disappointingly few contemporary references to Chippendale; the most enthusiastic (to 'that celebrated artist, Mr Chippendale of St Martin's Lane') appeared in a newspaper describing the 'very rich and most elegant ornamental' picture frame that he was said to have made for a portrait of the Duke of Northumberland – although it appears that this was not in fact his work. No obituaries were published on Chippendale's death, and for half a century the only surviving references to him were by a few fellow-professionals, who noted that his work was admirable but obsolete.

Curiously enough, Chippendale's legendary popular reputation, the result of some obscure groundswell of opin-ion, dates from the mid-19th century, when actual information about his life and work was becoming blurred or forgotten. Apart from the *Director*, there were few facts about Chippendale of which anyone could be sure, but he had become, and ever afterwards remained, a byword.

Scholarly opinion swung in the opposite direction. Understandably sceptical about an unsubstantiated greatness, historians began to question whether Chippendale was known in his own day, whether his work was outstanding, and, if so, whether the credit might not

Below: *Large writing table in the library at Stourhead, Wiltshire. The table is decorated with the carved heads of philosophers*

belong to skilled designers, who were perhaps truly responsible for the *Director*, and to architects such as Adam or the expert craftsmen who made Chippendale's furniture.

These doubts were perfectly valid, since there was no evidence that Chippendale was the creative hand and brain behind the *Director*, and it was impossible to determine which pieces of 18th-century furniture actually came from his workshop. Unlike their French fellow-craftsmen, English cabinet-makers failed to 'sign' their furniture with anything more substantial than printed paper labels, and many (Chippendale included) did not even bother with these. After time, circumstance and fashion had done their work for a few generations, destroying or dispersing the contents of houses, the number of pieces that could be attributed to any individual maker was lamentably small. Moreover, in terms of the best-known public patron Chippendale's achievement did not look impressive, since despite his excuses to Sir Rowland Winn there was no record of his having worked for the royal family. Several decades into the 20th century there were still reputable furniture historians finding plausible candidates for the design of 'Chippendale' designs and 'Chippendale' furniture.

But by this time the counter-attack had begun. Even now, few people realize that the 20th century is one of the great ages of scholarship, full of works that are imaginative, meticulous, and as near-exhaustive as it is in the nature of human endeavours to be. The

Above: *Chippendale chair c. 1780. From the Chippendale collection in the Victoria and Albert Museum*

quest for Thomas Chippendale could easily be written as a detective story, although the hero would not be a single master-sleuth but dozens of researchers whose discoveries have earned them little more than footnotes in later writings. Thanks to them, Chippendale was gradually brought into focus. Fragments of information concerning his life came to light in parish records. Investigations of his social and professional background in Yorkshire and London brought a greater understanding of his status and activities. Original drawings by Chippendale at last put his abilities as a designer beyond all reasonable doubt. And the gradual investigation of account books, bank records, legal documents, public notices, bills paid and unpaid, and correspondence provided an increasingly vivid picture of his professional life and, above all, the hard evidence needed to assign an ever-increasing number of pieces of furniture to Chippendale's workshop. Astonishingly, before 1906 there was no known documentary proof that *any* furniture had been made by him, although strong traditions and circumstantial evidence carried a good deal of weight in certain instances; whereas at present over 700 pieces are confidently attributed to Chippendale. Finally, even his claim to have worked for the royal family was authenticated when a suite of sofas and armchairs at Clarence House was added to the Chippendale canon.

'Chippendale' remains a name to conjure with. Authenticated works, still relatively few in number, rarely come on the market, but in auction rooms the prices of 'Chippendale style' and 'Chippendale period' furniture rise steadily, while 'American Chippendale' has achieved a startling popularity. As for the reputation of the master-craftsman, thanks to generations of collective scholarly effort that stands higher than ever today. But if most people are unaware of the change it is because, in a sense, nothing *has* changed: popular tradition has simply been proved absolutely right about the greatness of Thomas Chippendale.

Above: *Chimneypiece from the library at Nostell Priory which was remodelled by Adam in 1766 and is the most perfectly preserved of the rooms furnished by Chippendale*

INDEX

ACKNOWLEDGEMENTS

The publishers would like to thank the following for their kind permission to reproduce the illustrations in this book: British Library 30; Bridgeman Art Library 2, 15, 26, 32, 40, 44, 45TR, 53, 60, 63/4, 77, 96, 100, 106, 116;/Mallet & Sons 46TL, 48, 54TL, 54TR;/Victoria & Albert Museum 18, 37, 91, 103, 122; Christie's 4, 110, 111, 119; Country Life 82; Mary Evans Picture Library 11, 34; Angelo Hornak 20, 22, 23;/Sir Tatton Sykes Sledmere 46TR;/Harewood House 70, 71, 86; A.F. Kersting 28; Mansell Collection 61; National Portrait Gallery 24, 80, 83; National Trust Photographic Library/J. Gibson 10TL, 50, 56, 69, 73, 75, 93, 95, 101, 104, 105, 112, 113, 123;/J. Whitaker 12, 99;/A. Hornak 25; J. Bethell 68, 97, 108, 115, 121;/G. Shakerley 87; Octopus Group Picture Library 16, 35;/National Trust 58, 81;/Guildhall, Sun Alliance & London Insurance Group 59;/Victoria & Albert Museum 89;/Country Life & Earl of Pembroke 94; By Courtesy of the Trustees of Sir John Soane's Museum 85T; Spectrum Colour Library 8; By Courtesy of the Board of Trustees of the Victoria & Albert Museum 79; Derek G. Widdicombe 120; The Most Honourable the Marquess of Zetland/Photo: Eddie Ryle-Hodges 85B.